Liberalism

vs.

Conservatism

A Basic Guide to Understanding America's 21st Century Civil War

Freddy Davis

TSMPress

Liberalism vs. Conservatism: *A Basic Guide to Understanding America's 21ˢᵗ Century Civil War*

Copyright 2013 Freddy Davis

For Worldwide Distribution
Printed in USA

TSMPress
321 Anton Dr. • Tallahassee, FL 32312
850-383-9756

Table of Contents

Introduction

The guns have not started firing yet, but America is already in the middle of a new Civil War. This time, the great divide is not about states' rights and slavery, as in the previous war. This time, the split revolves around such things as abortion, homosexual marriage, gun control, religion in the public square, "right to die," pornography, drug use and the like. As it stands now, most people think of this conflict in terms of politics. However, the political arena is only one place where it plays out. There are many others.

In dealing with this subject, it seems that politics ought to be front and center. Certainly, in modern American culture, discussions about conservatism and liberalism usually center around politics. But to truly get at the guts of the topic, we have to go way beyond the political arena. To truly understand the war between conservatives and liberals, we have to probe at a deeper level.

Of course, we still have to explore the many ways people express liberal and conservative ideas in real life. After all, that is how we see the modern civil war taking place. But as important as it is to see and understand the various expressions of this war, understanding its root cause is even more critical. After all, it is knowing the origin of the conflicting beliefs that allows us to grasp the true nature of this modern war. When we understand the origin, we gain the ability to move beyond a simple awareness of the fact that it exists, to an understanding of "why" it exists and how to fight it.

We can find knowledge of the source of this war buried in a treasure chest called worldview. Worldview shows us how different people understand the structure of reality.

Now immediately, some will roll their eyes thinking we are getting ready to deal with some highfalutin academic study. But nothing could be further from the truth. It doesn't get more practical than this. Of course, any time we put ourselves in a position to learn something new, there is a learning curve we have to deal with. But in this case, it is worth every effort. Knowing about worldview will take you beyond simply trying to make sense of America's 21st century civil war. It will equip you to actually have an influence in the world.

Our worldview operates at such a core level of life that simply grasping the definitions only gets us started. A true apprehension of this topic takes us beyond definitions and opens up for us an understanding of the way other people actually view reality. And why is this so important? Because without understanding how people grasp reality, it is almost impossible to interpret what they mean when they speak – even if we understand their words.

The truth is, every one of us has a way we perceive reality. Even imagining reality as something other than what we already believe is very difficult. Thinking about a different reality has the feel of science fiction. After all, what we consider to be not real is, well, not real. So, when we begin interacting with people who literally understand reality differently than we do, making sense of their beliefs is nearly impossible. By the way, they will feel the same way about us. And that is exactly what we face when dealing with the conservative vs. liberal divide. But, when we understand worldview, everything comes into focus.

So, how does an understanding of the beliefs of liberals and conservatives help us? These are merely different political philosophies, right?

Actually, no! It is much more than that. It includes politics, of course, but what we are really looking at are different realities. It is these differences which cause people to have political (and other kinds of) divisions.

This book is an attempt to take that extra step. I don't want you to merely understand different political positions. Instead, I want you to have the ability to understand and compare the liberal and conservative foundations at a worldview level. With this, you will not only grasp "what" liberals and conservatives believe, you will also understand "why" they believe it.

It is my great hope that you will find this knowledge useful in a way that literally transforms your thinking. I hope it will give you a greater ability to interact intelligently with those you stand with and those you face in America's 21st century civil war.

Part I
What Does it Mean to Be Conservative and Liberal?

Chapter 1
What is Worldview?

"Lance, what are you doing here? I thought you had a meeting with your 'stupid conservative friends' today," Sally called out, with a giggle in her voice. Sally and Lance were really good friends and often hassled each other about their political beliefs.

Lance Jackson is a professor at the local university and teaches philosophy and religion. He is a tall, handsome guy with brown hair, a strong chin and quite an athletic build. He played football in his college days and continues to work out diligently to keep himself healthy and in shape. Liberals in this community tend to view conservatives as somewhat "unlearned." This, however, certainly does not characterize Lance. While he is a staunch conservative, he is widely regarded as one of the more well-grounded advocates for that point of view in the community. In fact, he is the current president of the Conservative Council on campus.

For her part, Sally Livingston is one of Lance's colleagues at the university and teaches history. She is very striking to look at and makes it a point to be noticed with her flaming red hair flowing in the wind and her always up-to-date wardrobe. As conservative as is Lance, Sally is an equally steadfast liberal. While liberals have a reputation among the conservative community for being a bit flaky, that term does not characterize Sally in the least. She is definitely one of the more thoughtful and intelligent members of her liberal community and is the current president of the campus Secular Humanist Society.

"Hey, liberal Sal," Lance chuckled back. "I'm on my way to a meeting of the Conservative Council right now. You don't have to worry about me being late. I lead the meeting so they can't start without me."

As they were both headed in the same direction, the two of them walked along together for a while. As they walked, they picked up the conversation where they had left off the last time they saw each other.

"Lance," Sally offered, "I just don't get why you fall for that conservative dribble. You are way too intelligent for that. You are not really like most of that conservative crowd at all, as far as I can tell. Seriously, what do you see in it?"

"Sally, your problem is that you operate too much off of stereotypes," Lance countered. "I am way more like all of them than you can even imagine. And they are way more intelligent than you give them credit for. You ought to actually come meet some of them. I think you will be surprised. Your problem is, you just don't understand the worldview basis for conservative beliefs."

As Sally contemplated what Lance had just said, she turned a bit more serious and said, "I do understand that worldview, Lance. It is just that the whole conservative foundation about God being an objectively real person that you can literally talk to is just stupid – no offense. Don't you realize that we now live in a day when science is able to explain reality in terms that make belief in God just silly?"

Lance stopped short and turned toward Sally to make his point more forceful. "Sally, you think you understand, but you really don't get it," Lance retorted. "I do realize that my conservative beliefs are founded on a faith foundation. But so are yours. What you are touting as a belief based on science is just as much a statement of faith as my belief about God. That is simply the nature of worldview beliefs."

After walking just a short distance more, they arrived at the place where Lance had to turn off to go to his meeting. "Hey, Sally, why don't you come to the meeting with me? I'm sure you will have a great time," Lance said as he signaled his intent to leave her.

Sally raised and crossed her arms in the form of an X and shot back, "Ugh! I don't think so today. It just seems to me such a waste of time. I'll tell you what though, I really do think it would be valuable to understand your beliefs better. Maybe we can carve out some time just for the two of us to give our best shot at converting each other."

Sally really thought what she said was funny and laughed out loud at the thought of trying to convince Lance that his beliefs were wrong. At that, Lance also thought it was funny and laughed with her. "You know," he replied, "I like that idea. I think I can help you find the truth." They both laughed some more and made arrangements to play phone tag the next week to set up a time.

They waved as they parted company, both knowing that they had better spend time preparing for the next encounter. Defending one's worldview is not something that you enter into without planning well.

****

Before diving too deeply into this book, you have to ask yourself one question: Do I really want to understand where liberal and conservative beliefs come from? If so, you are first going to have to step beyond mere pop culture definitions and explanations to learn about the topic of worldview. I hate to begin the book this way, but worldview is not yet a topic of everyday conversation. Because of that, there are not many places to go to get up to speed about it. That being said, it is where we have to go to understand the true nature of liberal and conservative beliefs. As we move deeper into the book, more outward expressions of this topic will emerge. But, we can't truly appreciate those "outward" parts without first getting a basic grasp of the topic itself.

Don't get me wrong. Some will find this initial plunge utterly fascinating. For me personally, I love this topic. On the other hand, there will be some who wonder why we are even talking about this stuff. This is where you have to trust me. Just go ahead and allow yourself to get your initial foundation. After you do, everything will begin to make sense in a way that couldn't happen without it. The truth is, no one can understand and appreciate any topic without a basic foundation.

We throw around the terms liberal and conservative so much these days that, in many ways, the words themselves have lost most of their meaning. In modern times, these words are more closely associated with particular political tribes than with the meanings of the words themselves. It has become much like the feud between the Hatfields and McCoys – everyone still feuds, but no one really knows what the fight is all about.

If we are going to deal intelligently with such a deep topic, the first thing we need to do is understand what, exactly, we are talking about. To do that, we must do more than just define words. We must come to understand the actual worldview foundations that the words represent.

The word "worldview" is becoming ever more common in modern times. That being said, it is one of those terms which has a familiar ring, but very few people are able to define with any precision. As such, most use the word as a kind of generic placeholder, rather than as something truly meaningful. Most people conceive of worldview as "the way people think," "the way people look at the world," a "philosophy of life," or a "point of view." These expressions may all be true to a certain extent, but none of them really tell us anything. These definitions are mostly fluff. But the truth is, the word "worldview" has a very precise meaning. Understanding this meaning is critical for those who want to get to the heart of the difference between conservative and liberal beliefs.

So, What is Worldview?

The word worldview itself is not that hard to define. That said, the idea that the word represents is difficult for most people to grasp. The reason for the difficulty is that it deals with people's very understanding of reality – that is, what they recognize to be real and unreal. What makes this even more complex is that, generally speaking, people are not even consciously aware of their own beliefs about reality. Beyond that, they tend to be even less aware of the beliefs of those who have a different worldview. In fact, it is difficult to even conceive that other people believe something is real that we consider to be unreal. How could they do that? Sure, people disagree about many things, but everybody at least has the same way they understand what is real, right? Unfortunately, the answer to that question is NO!

There is, in fact, only one way that reality is *actually* structured. The world objectively exists in a particular way and it doesn't exist any other way. That being said, there are various ways that different groups of people conceive of reality. These conflicting views are ultimately the root of the various clashes we observe in the culture. As we consider the clash between liberals and conservatives, the first thing we must grasp is that they operate from entirely different ways of understanding reality. Liberalism and conservatism are based on two different worldview foundations.

So, let's get right to the definition. *A worldview is a set of assumptions about the nature of reality*.

At first glance, this definition may seem a little academic and esoteric. But as we break it down, you will see that it is not as complicated as all that.

The phrase "set of assumptions" represents the first key concept in the definition. So, just what is an assumption? It is nothing more than a belief which seems so obvious it is hard to imagine anyone would question it. As such, assumptions are typically unconscious beliefs. We never question them. We just take them for granted. Worldview beliefs operate at this level.

The second key idea in the definition is "nature of reality." All we are talking about here is the way the universe actually exists. It actually exists in some form and does not exist in any other form. The fact that people with different worldviews have different beliefs about reality does not change the reality itself. Every person in the world lives life *as if* it exists the way they believe – whether they are right or not.

So, let's summarize the definition. A worldview is a set of beliefs about how reality is structured which seems so obvious, it is hard to imagine anyone would even question it.

Worldview Analogies

While knowledge of the definition of worldview is an essential starting point, we need a little more explanation to understand its deep implications. In order to probe a little deeper, let's look at four analogies which will help us gain a deeper insight into the definition.

A Worldview is Like an Environment

Pretend for a moment that you are a fish living in a pond in the middle of a forest. As it turns out, you are not only the smartest fish in the pond, you have this insatiable appetite to know all you can about the pond in which you live. So you have learned everything there is to know. You know all of the other fish that live there, as well as about all of the other kinds of animal and plant life. You know the shape and bottom features of the pond. You have even studied the pond's surroundings and observed the grass, trees and various wildlife that encircle it.

One day, while doing some observations, you heard a loud splash. Being the curious sort that you are, you swam over to where you heard the sound. When you got there, you received the shock of your life. Right there in front of you was another fish – but this was like no other fish you had ever seen.

Well, because of your insatiable curiosity, you swam up to this new specimen and began giving him the third degree. As you listened to his answers, he told you that he had lived in another pond, been caught, brought to this new one and thrown in. Your first shock came because you never conceived that other ponds even existed. Your amazement compounded as he told you of other kinds of fish and creatures that lived in his pond that you had never even imagined. It was truly hard to believe that things like what he was describing could actually exist.

A worldview is a *belief environment*. Like the pond in the forest, this environment is very exclusive. And as the smart fish was not aware of other ponds in other places, most people are only aware of the particular beliefs about reality that they were raised with. As such, when they hear of the existence of other worldview beliefs (environments), they don't have any way to evaluate them, so they don't make any sense. The natural reaction is, "How could anyone possibly believe that?"

A Worldview is Like a Lens

Imagine that when you were born, your mother put a pair of red glasses on your face. You had worn those glasses your entire life and had never seen anything that was not viewed through them. Under those circumstances, everything seen through the red lenses would look normal because that is all you had ever known.

If one day, though, you happened to put on a pair of glasses with uncolored lenses and looked through them, everything would look abnormal. This would be the case even though you would be seeing things the way they *actually* exist.

You would continue to live under this illusion until you could somehow come to the realization that the uncolored lenses show you actual reality. Until that realization hit you, you would continue to live life "as if" the red tinted glasses represented reality and would continue to believe that the clear ones actually skewed it.

A worldview is a set of belief lenses. People look through their worldview beliefs to understand how reality exists. If their own worldview beliefs do not represent actual reality, they simply don't know it and live life *as if* their beliefs were true – even though they are not.

Evaluating life through a belief lens which does not represent true reality will certainly cause people to have inner conflict as they rub up against the truth. But if they don't realize that their beliefs are wrong, they will simply not recognize what is causing the feelings of conflict. It is possible for people to live their entire lives filtering their experience through a false set of beliefs and actually think that their belief lens represents the Truth. But it doesn't alter the fact that it is not.

A Worldview is Like the Foundation of a Building

There are two aspects of the foundation of a building that are critical. Both of these define the boundaries of what is possible when a building is constructed.

The first is its shape. When a foundation is laid, its shape defines the building's possible outer boundaries. Trying to build outside of the foundation will lead to the building's collapse.

The second critical part of the foundation is its strength. The superstructure of the building can be made lighter than what the foundation will support, but not heavier. If the weight of the building is heavier than what the foundation can support, it will ultimately collapse.

A worldview is a belief foundation. It defines the outer limits of a person's beliefs and its strength.

First, it defines the shape of the belief system. Beliefs which do not fit on a particular worldview foundation belong to some other system. If other beliefs are allowed in, it results in internal contradictions which will ultimately cause chaos within a person's heart.

Secondly, the belief foundation determines the strength of the belief system. If there are contradictions, historical untruths or logical weaknesses within the system, it will ultimately fall apart because these conflicting beliefs don't support one another. This, too, will result in bedlam within a person's core.

A Worldview is Like a Language

If two people do not speak the same language, they will not understand one another when they try to communicate. Even if they are trying to communicate about the same topic and are both competent on that topic, communication will not occur if they are not able to bridge the language barrier.

A worldview is a belief language. The ideas people talk about are based on their understanding of reality. So, even if two people are using a common language, communication will be difficult if their worldview beliefs are different. That happens because the person hearing the speech will interpret the meaning of the words differently than the speaker intended.

Pulling it All Together

When I lived in Japan, I came to appreciate and enjoy many of the arts that were uniquely Japanese. One thing in particular that I enjoyed was origami – the Japanese art of paper folding.

One of my favorite forms is the flying bird. I can take a piece of paper and fold it in a way that makes it appear to be a bird. With one particular pattern, the wings will even flap when I pull its tail.

But when I make that paper figure, is it a real bird? Of course not! Although it has the form of a bird and can make a certain motion like a bird, it is still only a paper representation. Real birds are living creatures which are able to eat, procreate and fly.

Every worldview system which does not represent actual reality is like the paper bird. It can imitate the real thing in certain respects, but it is not real. Our ultimate desire must be to grasp true reality and base the way we live life upon it.

At this point, we could take our definition of worldview and go in several different directions. We could use this knowledge to gain a deeper understanding of religion, business methodologies, social practices or many other issues. But our purpose here is not to look at any of these areas. Rather, we want to use the concept of worldview to understand liberalism and conservatism. So now let's use the basic definition and images to explore how worldview beliefs are actually expressed in the real world.

Chapter 2
What are the Worldview Possibilities?

They hadn't planned to see each other quite so soon. However, it just so happened that as Sally was walking through the patio at the Student Union, she saw Lance sitting there reading some papers and drinking a bottle of water.

"Hey, conservo-man! What are you doing?" Sally shouted out as she walked up to his table.

"Libero-Sally! What's up? I have some time between classes and thought I would rather sit out here and get some fresh air than be cramped up in my office. Just grading some papers."

Sally didn't wait for an invitation, she just sat down in the chair across from him and started in. "I know you don't want to see me," she smirked. "You know that when you start trying to justify your conservative beliefs that I am going to blow you out of the water."

"Yeah, right! As if you knew enough about worldview beliefs to even walk in my presence," Lance parleyed. "You know I am one of the foremost experts on that topic in the world, right?"

"Hey, I'm not intimidated by you. I know what I believe and I can hold my own," Sally shot back. "But yeah, I know you are an expert in that field. In fact, before we begin meeting, I want to tap into your expertise. Since we are going to be dealing with our beliefs based on worldview rather than just political ideas, I wanted you to give me a brief overview of the topic from your perspective. I've read some of your stuff and it is very interesting. I know there are more beliefs out there than just the ones you and I hold. How 'bout giving me a brief tutorial. Do you mind?"

Lance put his papers down on the table and looked up, "You know I'm a sucker when it comes to talking about this stuff. It is where my passion is. You got a few minutes now?"

Both of them had classes to teach the next hour, but had a good thirty minutes before they had to be there. So, Lance took the opportunity to share some of the basics regarding worldview possibilities so that next time they met they could dive right in.

Before they left, Lance spoke up, "Hey, we haven't set a time and place to begin our discussions yet. How about next Thursday around noon at the diner near your office?"

"Yeah, I like that place. It will be perfect. See you next week then?" Sally responded.

"Absolutely! See you then," Lance replied as he headed on his way.

****

Before we are able to effectively look at the specific ways worldview effects people's daily lives, there is one more thing we need – a context. And the way to get at context is to know the worldview possibilities. Liberalism and conservatism don't exist in a vacuum, they exist on specific worldview foundations. In order to get a big picture understanding, we need to know what all of the foundational possibilities look like.

As we continue to lay the groundwork for understanding liberalism and conservatism in America, the first thing we must come to grips with is that these two viewpoints are not ends in themselves. They are expressions of two different worldview categories. While most of the time people think of the worldview categories in religious terms, they can be expressed in other ways, as well. So, before we get to the specifics of the liberal and conservative viewpoints, we need to understand the bigger picture into which they fit.

The worldview foundations for liberalism and conservatism are not the only worldview possibilities. There are actually four basic worldview categories: Naturalism, Theism, Animism and Far Eastern Thought. Every religion, cult and philosophy in existence is based on one of these four. American liberalism and conservatism represent two of these.

While the primary focus of this book is on liberalism and conservatism, grasping the larger context will make everything more understandable. Thus, we will go ahead and look at a brief explanation of all four worldviews. This will help us understand liberalism and conservatism within the context of the universe of possibilities. From that, we will see where they fit within the big picture, as well as how they compare with one another.

But before we get into the explanation of the four worldview possibilities, we need to grasp one other concept – worldview essentials. There is a line around every worldview (and, actually, every belief system, as well) which cannot be crossed and still remain within that worldview system. To define that line, there are three questions we need to ask. The answers to these questions define the boundaries of the worldview. Each worldview answers the questions in its own unique way. The three questions are:

1) What is the nature of ultimate reality? (Does God exist or not? If he does, what is he like? If not, what is the organizing principle of the universe?)
2) What is a human being? (Do humans have a spiritual part or are they purely natural animals? If there is a spiritual part, what is it like? If there is not, how can we account for the parts of humanity which cannot be understood by science?)
3) What is the ultimate that life has to offer and how it is achieved? (Is this life all there is or is there something beyond? If there is nothing beyond, what is the most people can get out of this life? If there is something beyond, how do humans tap into it and what is it like?)

As was said earlier, every worldview answers these essential questions in its own unique way. Answer any one of them in a different way and you have moved out of one worldview into something else. With this background, let's now look at the four worldview possibilities.

Naturalism
Naturalism is the belief that there is no such thing as a supernatural existence. Naturalists believe that the natural matter of the universe, which is eternal and evolving, is the only thing that exists.

Naturalistic Belief Systems
Some of the more prominent belief systems which are founded upon the naturalistic worldview include:

- Secular Humanism
- Atheism
- Agnosticism
- Skepticism
- Existentialism
- Marxism
- Positivism
- Postmodernism

How Naturalism Answers the Worldview Questions

To get at the core beliefs of Naturalism, we only need to discover how it answers the three essential worldview questions.

1) What is the nature of ultimate reality?

Naturalism assumes that there is no supernatural existence. All of reality is expressed within the natural universe.

2) What is the nature of a human being?

In Naturalism, human beings are merely animal creatures which have a highly evolved brain.

3) What is the ultimate life has to offer and how is it achieved?

The ultimate life has to offer, in Naturalism, is physical survival and personal fulfillment. Individuals achieve these by doing whatever they find necessary based on personal goals and life circumstances.

Implications of Naturalistic Beliefs

The foundational beliefs of Naturalism lead to particular conclusions as people live out their lives. Since Naturalists don't believe in a supernatural reality, they don't recognize the existence of a God who can reveal right and wrong. Thus, the only place moral values can possibly come from are human beings themselves. There is no such thing as objective right and wrong, good and evil. All morality is relative to a particular situation. So, if conditions or situations change, there is no compelling reason the culture's moral beliefs can't also be changed. What used to be right can become wrong and what used to be bad can become good – if the situation warrants it.

This does not mean that people who follow a naturalistic belief system are without moral beliefs. It is just that their morality is based on their own interpretation of right and wrong rather than upon values imposed from the outside.

Based on these core beliefs, we can easily see where Naturalists get their ideas about morality. Since the natural universe is all they believe exists, the natural creatures who are capable of thinking in moral terms – human beings – must create moral values to meet the perceived needs of their society. So, when people create values and norms, they are strictly functional elements created to meet those needs. And, of course, the people in society who have the most influence are the ones who get to make most of those choices.

Theism

The second worldview category is Theism. The basic assumption of Theism is that there exists an infinite and transcendent (supernatural) God who is the Creator and Sustainer of the material universe.

Theistic Belief Systems

Some of the major belief systems which are founded upon a theistic worldview include:
- Christianity
- The Way International
- The Unity School of Christianity
- Children of God (also known as The Family of Love)
- Jehovah's Witnesses
- The Church of Jesus Christ of Latter-day Saints (Mormons)
- Judaism
- Kabbalah
- Islam
- Baha'i
- Nation of Islam

How Theism Answers the Worldview Questions

As with all other worldview categories, getting at the basic beliefs of Theism involves finding its answers to the three essential worldview questions.

1) What is the nature of ultimate reality?

Theism is the belief that a transcendent God created and sustains the material universe based on his own purposes.

2) What is the nature of a human being?

Theists believe that human beings are creatures God intentionally created for his own purpose.

3) What is the ultimate life has to offer and how is it achieved?

Theism asserts that God is the one who defines the ultimate purpose of human life since he created it. This purpose will be different for each theistic belief system as each one has its own understanding of God and his purposes. Each also has its own belief about man's part in God's plan. To find out the purpose for any particular system, it is necessary to study it individually.

Implications of Theistic Beliefs

As we look at the way Theism explains reality, we see several important implications. These implications give us insight about what to expect from people who hold theistic beliefs.

The first implication is that the impact on culture tends to be both moral and positive. This evaluation is from the perspective of the belief system itself, not from those on the outside who might evaluate it differently. It is very possible that outsiders might look at a faith system and consider it to be bad. Nevertheless, believers will contend that the teachings come from God and are, thus, good.

Theistic beliefs also have a tendency toward legalism. This is not necessarily so, but it is the tendency. The reason is, Theists assume that God himself has revealed the beliefs and, thus, human beings must follow them. Based on this foundation, it is not unusual for believers to develop a codified list of "dos and don'ts" to live by.

Another implication of Theism is that it acknowledges both a spiritual and a physical part of reality which exists to fulfill a purpose. It also leads to a view of life that promotes meaning, establishes a specific "right" way to view morality and encourages the use of technology in a way which promotes goodness based on their viewpoint. After all, Theists believe God has revealed these things and provided the reasons for them.

Theists also believe it is right to struggle against the moral wrongs of the world and change them to conform to the instructions given by God. His revelation is, after all, his will for mankind.

Finally, Theistic belief systems claim to receive direction from God, who is good and directs his followers to act that way as well. Thus, it is important for human beings to acknowledge God's ways and follow them.

Special Note

The worldview foundations of liberalism and conservatism, in America, are based primarily on the two worldviews represented above. However, as was mentioned before, we need to show all of the worldview possibilities in order to understand the broader context. This wider explanation gives us a way to more fully understand liberalism and conservatism within the universe of possibilities. As such, we will now look at the other two basic worldview categories – Animism and Far Eastern Thought.

Animism

The basic assumption of Animism is that the universe contains both material and immaterial parts. Spirits exist in a separate place from physical beings, but they interact with humans in an interdependent relationship. Humans on earth offer sacrifices and perform rituals which benefit the spirits. They, in turn, take care of the needs of humans on earth.

Animistic Belief Systems

The primary belief systems which are founded upon an animistic worldview include:
- Japanese Shinto
- Voodoo/Santeria
- Wicca
- Native American Religions
- Non-American Tribal Religions
- Paganism and Neo-Paganism
- Astrology
- Fortunetelling
- Spiritism

How Animism Answers the Worldview Questions

To understand the essential elements of Animism, we need to discover how it answers the three essential worldview questions.

1) What is the nature of ultimate reality?

Animists believe that many gods/spirits exist in the spirit world. They believe these spirits interact symbiotically with human beings in the physical world.

2) What is the nature of a human being?

In animistic thought, human beings are believed to be essentially spirit beings who are housed in a physical body during their life on earth. Animists believe that at physical death, a human's spirit enters the spirit world and lives the rest of its existence there.

3) What is the ultimate life has to offer and how is it achieved?

In Animism, the ultimate aim of human beings is to live physical life without oppression. They accomplish this by living in harmony with the spirits in the spirit world.

Implications of Animistic Beliefs

There are several important implications for the lives of those who follow an animistic worldview. For Animists, the world, and life in general, is not moving toward a higher destination. They, basically, think of life on earth as an eternal "present." As such, they tend to simply live life one day at a time and accept things the way they are. There is not a lot of planning for the future or striving to figure out how to solve complex problems.

Whenever anything "bad" happens, Animists generally see it to be the result of an offended spirit. The solution for overcoming this kind of problem is to locate the offended deity and offer prayers and offerings. Animists generally have no compulsion to overcome obstacles in life by looking for some kind of new solution. The impact on culture from that mentality is that there is no built-in inner drive to strive toward higher levels of achievement, either individually or as a society.

Far Eastern Thought

The impersonal life force is the essential core of the Far Eastern Thought (FET) worldview. This life force exists beyond the material universe, so it is supernatural. At the same time, it is not personal so cannot be characterized as God. In some ways it can be thought of as a kind of spiritual or living energy field. FET holds that pieces of the life force have spun off from the central core and are constantly working their way back with the ultimate end to re-merge with it.

In FET, everything in the physical universe is nothing more than pieces of the life force which have spun far enough away from the main body that they have taken on a different appearance. While its true existence is immaterial and impersonal, it appears to us who live in the material universe to be material and personal. When it ultimately returns to its origin, it will also return to its actual form.

For these spun off pieces of the life force to work back to their origin, they must cycle through many incarnations. Lower life forms have further to go and require more incarnations to reach the level where they can jump back to their origin. Higher life forms are closer to the jumping-off point.

To make progress in this reincarnation process, the life force, at whatever stage in the cycle, must live its life in a way that accumulates good karma. If it does well, it will move to a higher form in its next incarnation. When it makes it to the highest level and does well, the material reincarnations cease and the life force re-merges with the impersonal main body.

The FET worldview is characterized by two core philosophical concepts. First it is monistic. Monism is the belief that everything in all of reality consists of the same substance – in this case, the impersonal life force. Secondly, it is pantheistic. That is, everything in existence is divine because it is all made up of pieces of the ultimate reality – the impersonal life force.

FET Belief Systems

As with the other worldview categories, there are many major belief systems within the FET worldview. Among them are:

- Hinduism
- Buddhism
- Krishna

- Transcendental Meditation
- Jainism
- Sikhism

How FET Answers the Worldview Questions

As was true concerning the previous worldview systems, an understanding of FET requires that we discover how it answers the three essential worldview questions.

1) What is the nature of ultimate reality?

FET understands ultimate reality to be an impersonal life force which exists beyond the material universe. The universe, even though it is made up of pieces of the impersonal life force, appears different from its actual existence. It appears to contain material and personal elements. That, however, is an illusion. Ultimate reality is not material or personal. Everything, in all of existence, is made up of some expression of the impersonal life force.

2) What is the nature of a human being?

Human beings, in FET, are one of the higher expressions of the impersonal life force which exist in the material universe. While all life forms are expressions of the life force, human beings exist at a particular stage in the reincarnation cycle which seems self-conscious and personal. This, however, is an illusion since all of ultimate reality is impersonal.

3) What is the ultimate life has to offer and how is it achieved?

The ultimate that life has to offer, in FET, occurs when the pieces of the life force are finally able to reunite with the main body. They do this by reincarnating over many lifetimes to higher and higher levels until finally reaching the jumping off point. For human beings, the ultimate goal is to live the current life in a way that accumulates good karma. This allows the life force to advance to a higher level in its next life.

Implications of FET Beliefs

There are several important implications for the lives of those who believe the FET worldview. These implications greatly affect how people conceive of and live their lives.

One important belief is that, based on the principle of karma, people are born into their proper place in life. As such, everyone should be content in their life situation. This contentment does not necessarily mean they will experience pleasure or happiness with their lives. Rather, they simply recognize that the life situation they were born into is established and there is no hope of moving to another. Thus, there is no point in struggling to move outside their proper place in life.

Another implication is that nothing people experience in material life is a true expression of reality. True reality is impersonal. So, while they experience all manner of suffering in their lives, the life of suffering is not actual reality. Rather than fighting against their suffering, resigned endurance is the proper attitude to hold.

The primary impact of FET on culture is to promote a type of passivism that encourages people to be content in their life situation. That is, individuals within society should resign themselves to live life in the situation in which they were born.

Chapter 3
Worldview Foundations for
Conservatism & Liberalism

"Sally, good to see you again," Lance shouted out as he walked up to her table at the diner. "How is everything going with you and your liberal cohorts?"

Sally laughed at his greeting as he approached the table and sat down. He always did have a great sense of humor even if she didn't like his politics. "I'm doing great. How's everything with your conservative galoots?"

"Galoots? You are so funny. You can't get away from your awful stereotypes, can you?" Lance replied over his laughing. "If anyone is a galoot it is your liberal friends."

Before getting into any kind of deep discussion, they each ordered a burger and just talked about what was going on with their classes while they waited for their food.

After the waitress finally brought the food, Lance turned the conversation to the topic at hand. "Sally, are you really sure you understand what conservatives believe? I mean, really understand? Many of the comments you make about me and my beliefs seem not to be fully in sync with what I actually believe."

"Of course I do, Lance," Sally retorted as she set her burger down to give him her undivided attention. "I know that the differences we have are much deeper than politics. They really do go down to the level of our very worldviews."

"I believe you are absolutely right Sally," Lance replied as he set his drink down and looked her straight in the eye. "We really do look at reality through quite different lenses. So, what exactly do you think I believe?"

"Lance, I already know a good bit of your story. You grew up just over in the next county and got married to Linda right after you finished college. You guys have two kids – who are just adorable, by the way. And, I know that you are very active in that Christian church over on the other side of campus. You are so straight laced . . ."

"Straight laced?" Lance interrupted her. "What do you mean by that?"

Sally laughed out loud again. She was having fun with this. "Oh, don't take it badly," she said as she gave him one of those sideways glances. "I just know that your worldview perspective is based on Christian Theism and that you are very serious about it, that's all. I don't know how you can really believe all of that superstitious mumbo jumbo, but I know you do." Sally paused a moment then continued, "So, how do you evaluate my beliefs?"

"Oh, that's easy," Lance shot back as he smiled and leaned back against the padded vinyl seat. "In addition to having known you personally for all this time, I do keep up with your involvement in the local humanist society. Ever since you have taken over leadership of the group you have made sure that you guys stay very high profile. I even saw the article the campus paper did on you last year. They were pretty thorough. You are single, having been divorced. You don't have any kids and your job here at the university is your life. You are a hard core Naturalist. More specifically, you believe in the tenets of Secular Humanism. You consider yourself an Atheist and believe that morality is relative. Does that peg it pretty well?"

"Well, I would say that you have definitely done your homework. I am quite flattered that you've shown that much interest in me and will take that as a compliment," Sally responded as she, too, leaned against the back of the seat.

At that, Lance and Sally spent the next forty five minutes discussing the difference between Theism and Naturalism. Both found it very satisfying to have a conversation with someone who actually understood, in depth, what made the other tick.

****

Okay, now we can start getting to the good stuff. Unfortunately, we needed to wade through all of the foundational information before getting here. But as we move forward, you will see how everything else depends on that base.

In generic terms, conservatism and liberalism do not have a specific worldview foundation. That is because viewpoints are conservative or liberal in relation to something. They are not, in themselves, unique, identifiable categories. Thus, when we relate conservatism and liberalism to worldview, we must first identify their specific historical context.

In general terms, conservatism is a point of view which attempts to preserve what already exists. The desire to "conserve" the status quo is what makes it conservative. Liberalism, on the other hand, is a point of view which attempts to move beyond what already exists into a new direction. It is the desire to "liberate" from the status quo. Thus, what is liberal and conservative in one context will be different in another depending on the default historical position.

As we look at conservatism and liberalism in this book, we will focus on what it means in the context of Western culture generally, and American culture more specifically. To do this, we must first have some historical context.

Conservatism

America was founded upon a Theistic worldview. The particular form of Theism which underlies conservatism in America is Christian Theism. Sometimes people refer to this as the Judeo-Christian ethic.

In general terms, Theism has some form of scripture as its primary authority source. It is based on the belief that God has revealed himself and his ways to mankind. In the case of Christian Theism, the scriptural authority source is the Bible. Not only does this provide the foundation for America's moral and social expressions, it also advances the notion of a transcendent authority (God) that people should follow and obey.

Those who initially settled and developed American society were primarily Europeans who came from a Christian theistic worldview background and believed in the God of the Bible. As such, they established society's various institutions using ideas which came specifically from Christian Theism. Such concepts as the rule of law, freedom of conscience and individualism all came from this worldview foundation.

Obviously, these ideas can be codified in law and expressed in the culture in many ways. In the case of America's establishment, the founding fathers deliberately used ideas based on Christian Theism to create the system which now exists in America. It included:

- a constitution (an authoritative, foundational legal document),

- free enterprise (priority of the individual in economic matters),
- federalism (decentralized political power),
- separation of powers (recognition of the corruption that can come with power because of the moral weakness of human beings),
- property ownership (priority of the individual regarding land ownership), and
- freedom of religion (free will and freedom of conscience).

As such, the conservative position, as it relates to American culture, expresses the nation's founding principles. Conservatives are those who hold the point of view that these founding principles are right. These are the people who are working to preserve these principles in modern culture.

Liberalism

Liberalism, in America, has its root in the naturalistic worldview. The origin of this worldview belief goes far back into ancient times. We even see expressions of it in writings which date from ancient Greece. However, the modern understanding of Naturalism emerged out of the European enlightenment of the 18th and 19th centuries. This was a time when European culture was moving away from a God centered foundation to man centered one.

The naturalistic worldview framework was greatly advanced when Charles Darwin introduced his Theory of Evolution. This gave those inclined to naturalistic thinking a scientific sounding way to conceive of a reality which did not need God. From this base, Naturalism emerged as an increasingly influential belief platform. Politically, it took the form of communism, socialism and progressivism.

Naturalism expanded its influence in American culture as the number of people who believed in this worldview concept gradually increased. From the late 1800s through the 1950s, people with this belief foundation progressively worked their way into important positions within the culture's most influential institutions. By the 1960s, the liberal influence began to dominate in education, the news media and the entertainment industry. It was also well established in the nation's political institutions – in all branches and at all levels. Since the 1960s, the influence of liberalism has only increased.

The expansion of Naturalism has increasingly pushed Theism aside and caused American society to take on an entirely different character than that originally established by the founders. The basic authority source of Naturalism is human reason. As such, for liberals, it is not the outside authority of a god who provides the basis for personal and societal activity. Rather, since they do not believe in a transcendent, authoritative God, the people in positions of influence must make the rules. These powerful people use societal forces along with their personal preferences to influence how morality is defined within the culture. Along with that, they understand morality to be relative to current circumstances rather than absolute based on a revelation from God.

Another important liberal belief, which emerges out of Naturalism, is the priority of the collective – as opposed to the individual. Since liberals believe humans are completely natural animals, they think that the survival of the species, as a collective group, is more important than the development of the individual. Liberals in American culture tend to prefer institutional forms which are more consistent with a naturalistic worldview.

The language of liberalism has come to be expressed in modern culture using the notion of political correctness. Political correctness is the expression of language, ideas, policies, and behavior which tries to minimize giving offense to others. This kind of language is often found in common speech when speaking of occupation (flight attendant vs. stewardess), gender (firefighter vs. fireman), race (Native American vs. Indian), culture (holiday tree vs. Christmas tree), sexual orientation (gay vs. homosexual), religion (spiritually challenged vs. sinful), disability (intellectually challenged vs. retarded), and age (gerontologically advanced vs. elderly). The purpose of this kind of language is to minimize the differences between individuals in order to create more unity within the collective. Liberals believe doing this promotes the survival of the collective.

Conservatism and Liberalism in the Current American Climate

As we can see, conservatism and liberalism are not merely opposing political philosophies. They certainly do include political differences, but the roots go much deeper. On the most fundamental level, they are conflicting worldviews which literally contradict one another. They are ways of bringing order to society which view reality in completely different terms. The culture war battles, which the clash between conservatism and liberalism represent, are not mere matters of preference. They are expressions of deeply held fundamental beliefs.

While conservatism and liberalism are not, themselves, religious positions, the worldview foundations they rest upon are fundamentally religious in nature. As such, these expressions will continue to create a great deal of passion and division as they play out in every part of life.

Comparison of Liberal and Conservative Values

As we saw earlier while defining the worldview categories, Christian Theism and Naturalism have very specific beliefs about God, man and the ultimate that humans can expect out of life. These beliefs do not exist in a vacuum and are not merely personal preferences. They are, literally, different ways of understanding how reality exists.

As such, the expressions of these beliefs are also very specific. We can easily see how they are displayed in American culture. They result in a massive clash of cultural values which cannot be easily reconciled. Ultimately, one will dominate and put the other in a subservient position. The following chart shows, side-by-side, some of the more prominent ways these values compare with each other and how they are expressed in the culture.

Conservative Values (Based on Biblical Theism)	Liberal Values (Based on Naturalism)
Man is essentially sinful - The belief, based on a biblical understanding of the nature of mankind, that societal constraints must be in place to lessen the effects of sin.	**Man can build utopia on earth** - The belief, based on the concept of naturalistic evolution, that man has already evolved to a high form and will continue on that path. Social engineering can enhance the evolution of the goodness of man.

Conservative Values (Based on Biblical Theism)	Liberal Values (Based on Naturalism)
Natural law - The belief that there are such things as unchanging natural and moral laws which God has established for man to know and follow.	**Positive law** - The belief that man-made laws are responsible for bestowing or removing specific privileges from an individual or group. There is no God, so humans must make these laws themselves.
Constitutional authority - The belief that there is an overarching, authoritative legal framework which is the ultimate foundation for all other laws. This corresponds to the biblical concept of an authoritative document given by God.	**Human authority** - The belief, based on naturalistic concepts, that the highest authority is man. Those in power positions within society may create and alter laws based on their perception of current circumstances.
Free enterprise - The belief, based on biblical teachings, that individuals should work hard and be rewarded for their labor in a free economic environment.	**Economic collectivism** - The belief, based on naturalistic presuppositions, that human survival is the highest value, and equal distribution of resources best promotes that in society.
Individual property ownership - The belief, based on the biblical concept of stewardship and the priority of the individual, that people should hold personal property and be responsible to God for its use.	**Collective ownership of property** - The belief, based on the naturalistic concept of the survival of the species and the priority of the collective, that corporate ownership of property best promotes the interests of society.

Conservative Values (Based on Biblical Theism)	Liberal Values (Based on Naturalism)
Freedom of religion - The belief, based on the biblical concept that human beings are free-will creatures created in the image of God, that individuals should make life decisions based on freedom of conscience.	**Individual religious belief is subservient to the collective** - The belief, based on the naturalistic concept that human beings are naturally evolved animal creatures, that governmental leadership is best able to decide what promotes the survival of the collective.
Federalism - The belief, based on the biblical concept of the sinfulness of man and the priority of the individual, that governmental power ought to be decentralized.	**Centralized federal authority** - The belief, based on the naturalistic concept of the priority of the collective, that concentrated political power most effectively promotes the survival of social groupings.
Separation of powers - The belief that political power ought to be diluted, based on the biblical concept that human beings are sinful and that concentrated power allows the moral weakness of man to disadvantage the population at large.	**Concentration of power** - The belief that centralized political power is best able to promote the survival of society, based on the naturalistic concept that the collective has priority over the individual.

Chapter 4
Cultural Expressions of Conservatism and Liberalism

When they last met, Lance and Sally decided they would really get into it the next time. They decided that with each other they would throw caution to the wind. Sally, especially, was ready to show Lance how his narrow-minded point of view could not be defended. Lance, for his part, was confident of his position and felt that Sally wasn't going to know what hit her when they got into the nuts and bolts of the conversation. On the last occasion they decided they would meet on Thursdays for lunch at the same diner where they met before. Neither had classes to teach on Thursday afternoons, so it was a good time for both of them.

The next week, Sally got there first and got a booth back in the corner where they were less likely to be interrupted. She knew that Lance would want a bottle of water, so she went ahead and got menus from the waitress and ordered him a water and herself a glass of tea. Just as the waitress was leaving, Lance walked up.

"Hey Sally," Lance called out, "you sure got here quickly."

"Yeah," Sally replied. "I didn't have as far to go as you. My last class is in the building right next door."

"Well, that makes it easy, doesn't it? Have you ordered yet?" Lance asked as he got himself settled in.

"Not yet. I did order you a bottle of water, though. I figured that is what you would want since that's what you always get."

"Perfect," Lance replied back.

Just then the waitress returned with their drinks. "Do you guys know what you want yet?" she asked as she pulled out her order pad.

"I think I'll have a chicken sandwich and fries," Sally answered.

Lance looked up at her and asked, "How big are your burgers?"

Without hesitation the waitress replied, "We have 1/3 pound and 1/2 pound patties."

"Great," Lance responded. "Give me a 1/3 pound burger with sweet potato fries."

The waitress had no sooner stepped away than Sally jumped right in. "Lance, how in the world can you conservatives be so insensitive and narrow minded? Let me just give you a short list. You don't believe that a woman should have a right to do what she wants with her own body, you believe gays who love each other should not be able to marry, you think it is okay for just anyone to have a gun, even with all of the killings we have these days, you are so prudish when it comes to sexual activity, you don't think adults should be allowed to make their own decisions about smoking weed. . . . Good grief! Why do you want to put such heavy restrictions on everybody? Why not just let people do what they want?"

At that, Lance threw up his hand to settle Sally down a bit. "Whoa, Sally, calm down," Lance said, furrowing his brow. "Do you have any idea what you are really saying with all of these accusations? Every single thing you are talking about has another side. Do you realize that a baby is murdered every time a woman 'chooses' to abort? Do you realize the social and freedom issues that go along with gay marriage? Do you not know that the places with the strictest gun laws have the highest gun murder rates? I could go on, but my point is that there is another side to every issue you have brought up."

"I know that Lance, but what makes your beliefs the ones that should be followed?"

"Uh, Sally, what makes yours the right ones?" Lance shot back.

"Well, I guess that's what it ultimately gets down to, doesn't it?" Sally replied. "How do we know what is the right thing to do?"

Just then the waitress came and brought their food. "You guys need anything else?" she asked. Both of them shook their heads and thanked her as she finished putting their plates on the table and turned to walk away.

Lance immediately picked back up where the conversation had left off. "How, indeed, do we know?"

For the next forty five minutes they talked about almost every issue under the sun. There was hardly anything in the world that they agreed on – that is, except that the food at the diner was really tasty.

****

Societies must deal with many issues, both at the individual and collective level. Virtually all have some moral component attached to them. Since each worldview deals with this its own way, conservatives and liberals will have different beliefs about how to grapple with them. These different beliefs lead to the battles which are fought within a culture. The lists below are not exhaustive, but do represent the major categories and topics where people are fighting the culture war battles.

Life Issues
Topics Generally Associated with Life

Abortion	Population control	"Right to die"
Euthanasia	Murder	Terrorism
Suicide	Gun control	War
Genocide	Right to self-defense	Animal rights

Conservative Belief

Conservative beliefs are based on biblical assumptions which aggressively promote the sanctity of human life. One key principle is that the murder of innocents is not acceptable. That being said, there are cases where taking a life is acceptable, though conservatives always consider it unfortunate. Even so, no acceptable taking of life involves the taking of innocent life. Abortion, euthanasia, suicide, genocide, "right to die" issues, murder, and terrorism all fit into the "innocent life" category. Places where the taking of life may be permitted include self-defense, war, and the government's exercise of proper justice.

Conservatives also believe human life has priority over other life forms. They believe God specially created human beings in his own image. This cannot be said of other life forms. That does not mean other life is without value. Based on the biblical principle of stewardship, human beings ought to respect and take care of the entire created order. This does not imply, however, that the killing of other life forms is wrong, in and of itself. It is just that it must fit within the overall belief revealed in the Bible.

Liberal Belief

Based on liberal beliefs, there is no such thing as an objective right or wrong regarding life issues. That is because liberalism does not recognize the existence of a transcendent moral agent (God) who is able to declare them so. Each issue in the list above is considered good or bad depending on the needs of society at any given moment and in any given circumstance. As such, even the taking of "innocent" life can be justified in particular situations.

On the other side of the ledger, under certain circumstances, liberals may consider it unacceptable to take a life even if an individual has committed some serious offense. Everything depends on how society judges it to promote its survival.

Additionally, liberals believe other life forms are just as valuable as human life. Naturalists believe that every life form, including human beings, are merely living creatures which have naturally evolved to their current state. Many go so far as to assert that humans should advocate for nonhuman life in the same way they advocate for human life in order to promote the survival of natural life on earth.

Sexual Issues
Topics Generally Associated with Sexuality

Adultery	Fornication	Pornography
Bigamy	Homosexuality	Rape
Polygamy	Pedophilia	Prostitution
Exhibitionism	Bestiality	

Conservative Belief

Based on the teachings of the Bible, conservatives believe proper sexual activity only exists within the context of a sacred spiritual union between one man and one woman. They believe God designed sexual relations to be exercised only within the bonds of marriage, and any sexual activity outside the marriage relationship is considered wrong.

Additionally, improper sexual activity also degrades others by casting them as objects rather than persons made in the image of

God. Conservatives believe objectifying people is the wrong way to think of other humans who are God's special creations.

Liberal Belief

Since liberalism has no belief in an objective transcendent morality (morality given by God), liberals regard no sexual practice to be wrong, in and of itself. They would evaluate each situation as good or bad depending on personal preferences and the needs of society at any given moment and in any given circumstance.

Personal Integrity Issues
Topics Generally Associated with Personal Integrity

Cheating	Profanity	Theft
Fraud	Lying	Revenge
Greed		

Conservative Belief

The Bible teaches a standard of holiness that is based on the character of God. This standard is the basis for a conservative understanding of reality. So, participating in the activities on this list would cause individuals to act contrary to the character of God. As such, conservatives consider each of these things to be wrong.

Liberal Belief

Most liberals would probably also frown on someone who lived life by engaging in this list's activities, in most circumstances. The reason for considering them bad, however, is very different from that of the conservatives. In the case of naturalistic belief, these things would be wrong only to the degree they harm society. As liberals believe there is no such thing as an objectively true morality, nothing can be considered right or wrong in and of itself. There may actually be instances when any one of these practices might be considered no problem at all. Their rightness or wrongness is totally relative to the particular situation.

Physical Health Issues
Topics Generally Associated with Physical Health

Alcohol abuse	Obesity	Physical Exercise
Drug abuse	Smoking	Access to healthcare
Gluttony	Overwork	Pollution

Conservative Belief

Based on the teachings of Christian Theism, conservatives have a high view of the value of the human body. They consider a person's body to be the "temple of the Holy Spirit," which is the dwelling place of God in this world. As such, conservatives believe it is wrong to do anything which will cause the body to be less effective in carrying out God's purposes.

Liberal Belief

Since liberals believe the preservation of life is the highest possible value, anything which degrades life can be problematic. While this principle applies to all life forms, human beings have a particular interest in the survival of their own species. As such, liberals generally believe it is a bad thing to participate in activities which potentially destroy the self. It is not that any particular issue on this list can be considered innately immoral, since morality is relative to the situation. Particular issues can only be considered bad to the degree they compromise the survival of the social order.

Industriousness Issues
Topics Generally Associated with Industriousness

Gambling	Begging	Laziness
Hedonism	Mooching	

Conservative Beliefs

The teachings of the Bible suggest that a person's lifestyle is of utmost importance. Based on these teachings, conservatives believe the most important passion for any individual should be to please God, not self. This requires that human beings live life in ways which actively accomplish God's purposes. Participating in the activities on the above list generally works against that goal. For conservatives, creating a lifestyle which puts aside industriousness breaks down the fellowship a person is able to experience with God and completely counteracts God's purposes for mankind.

Liberal Beliefs

Based on naturalistic presuppositions, liberals consider human life to have ultimate value. As such, they generally regard participation in activities which could damage society to be a bad thing. It is not that any one of these activities are considered innately immoral, since morality is relative to particular circumstances. They are only considered bad to the degree they compromise the survival of the social order.

Relationship Issues
Topics Generally Associated with Human Relationships

Bigotry	Hatred	Prejudice
Child Exploitation	Marriage	Slavery
Domestic Violence	Divorce	Torture

Conservative Beliefs

Based on the teachings of the Bible, conservatives have a high view of the value of the individual and the family. They consider any activity which degrades other individuals or promotes the breakdown of the family to be problematic. Conservatives believe people should deal with all of the issues in this category in ways which promote the kind of relationships approved by God in his revelation.

Liberal Beliefs

Based on naturalistic presuppositions, liberals do not consider any of the issues listed in this category to be right or wrong in and of themselves. Each one is evaluated as good or bad depending on the needs of society at any given moment and in any given circumstance. Any of these issues which strengthen one's own group at the expense of an enemy could be considered good. On the other hand, some of them may cause a weakening within one's own group and might be considered wrong on that front.

Church-State Issues
Topics Generally Associated with Church-State Issues

Religious organizations meeting on public property	Religious symbols included in public symbols	Religious words in the pledge of allegiance
Religious symbols on public property	Government money to religious schools	Posting of Ten Commandments
Praying at public institutions	Government money to religious charities	Praying in school
Homeschooling		

Conservative Beliefs
Even within Christian Theism there is a variety of opinion about particular issues in this category. In America, however, most people would prefer that individuals be free to express their religious beliefs in the public square. This can be done without the state approving the expressions as official government policy. Generally, conservatives make a distinction between an individual's expression of his or her religion in the public square and the state actually establishing an official religious position.

Liberal Beliefs
Typically, liberals take issue with mixing "religion" with public life because they see it as pointless. They view any acceptance of spiritual reality as superstition. The truth is, although most Naturalists do not consider themselves religious, naturalism is a faith position and, therefore, a religious movement. This religion, though, is secular/atheistic in nature. Generally, naturalists object to any religious expression that recognizes the existence of God or to any non-empirical approach to understanding reality.

Chapter 5
Who are the Conservatives and Liberals?

Sally was not able to meet the next week as she had some important responsibilities to take care of with one of her students. When she called Lance to let him know, she suggested that they just pick up the following week – same time, same station. Lance was good with that, so they skipped a week and met again the following Thursday.

While they disagreed on practically everything, they were becoming comfortable enough with each other's positions that they were able to dispense with most of the formalities. Now they were just getting into it as soon as they sat down. So the following Thursday when they met, they gave their orders to the waitress and jumped right in.

But just when they were starting to hit their stride, Dell walked up. Dell was a fellow professor and a good friend with both of them, so he didn't even ask but simply plopped himself down next to Lance and said, "You guys don't mind if I eat with you, do you? I didn't think so." Then he turned toward where the waitress was standing and shouted over to her, "Ma'am, would you bring me the number two combo with a diet cola? Thanks."

Lance and Sally looked at each other, rather shocked that Dell would intrude that way, and wondered what to do. Then Dell asked, "What are you guys talking about?" At that, Sally told Dell about their conversation and caught him up a little on what they had been saying.

Normally, Dell was not really into that kind of conversation. He thought both of them were too extreme. "You know, guys," Dell said as he looked at one and then the other, "both of you need to get a life. Sally, I'm with you about abortion, gay marriage and smoking weed. The government needs to stay out of our lives."

With that, Sally perked up. She had herself an ally and would now be able to beat up on Lance with a little more force.

But Dell didn't stop talking. "Lance," he continued, "I agree with you when it comes to being fiscally conservative. The government is literally ruining the country with these out of control entitlement programs. And I don't even know what to say about that dad-gummed federal reserve!"

At that, both Lance and Sally were dumbfounded. They looked at each other, then at Dell, and at the same time blurted out, "Huh?"

Sally then shot back, "Dell, how can you say that. You have a very good liberal position on social issues, then you run off the track when it comes to government finances. Don't you think that the government ought to be helping those in society who are in need? Don't you think the rich are taking advantage of the poor and ought to pay their fair share?"

"Sally," Dell objected, "how can you say that? The rich are already getting soaked. Who do you think are the ones able to provide jobs for the poor? Are other poor people going to do it? Heck no! You are just messed up on that."

Then Lance chimed in, "But Dell, why are you conservative when it comes to fiscal policy but liberal when it comes to social issues?"

"That's just what's right," Dell answered back, "pure and simple."

The conversation didn't go anywhere after that. There was too much history with Lance and Sally to go back over all of the points they had already talked about. And to boot, Dell had thrown too many variables into the mix for the conversation to get back on track. So, they just changed the subject and talked about school for the rest of the meal.

When they had finished eating, Dell got up as abruptly as he had come in. "Hey, enjoyed eating with you guys. I'll talk to you later." And with that he left.

It was too late to get back into the conversation now, so they decided to just pick it up again the next week. "Lance," Sally suggested, "if Del comes again in the future and interrupts us, let's be just be as strong as he was and tell him we are having a private conversation?"

"Yeah, I think you're right." Lance responded. "We won't let that happen again."

With that, the two parted company. "See you next week, Sally."

"Super, Lance. Look forward to it," Sally responded. "It'll be better next week."

****

It is one thing to simply define conservatism and liberalism. It is another thing altogether to identify the people who fit into these categories. The truth is, there is not a truly foolproof way to do that. In modern society, we find a tremendous amount of hybridization when it comes to worldview perspectives. As you have read the various explanations written here about liberalism and conservatism, you probably sometimes thought, "I'm a liberal and I don't agree with that," or, "I'm a conservative and that's not the way I think."

Pay careful attention, here. If these kinds of thoughts came to mind as you were reading, you have already missed the point. Remember, the intent of this explanation is not to identify your personal leanings. You may very well have hybridized your personal beliefs so that your individual philosophy contains both liberal and conservative (theistic and naturalistic) elements. Rather, the point here is to identify the *origin* of the various beliefs themselves. At that point, it becomes possible to intelligently decide for yourself what you want to believe, rather than just "falling" into beliefs without knowing why you have them.

The truth is, for those who are solidly committed to one side or the other (those who have an ideological understanding and connection to pure Christian Theism or Naturalism), it is not at all difficult to understand why particular beliefs are affirmed. However, the vast majority of people, for various reasons, identify with certain elements of both sides. This hybridization tends to make many people wishy-washy and unpredictable in their beliefs. It also makes it difficult to precisely categorize these individuals as liberal or conservative. Hopefully, an understanding of the sources of the various worldview beliefs will help. At the very least it ought to clear up a certain amount of personal confusion.

Ideological Conservatives

Ideological conservatives tend to be very solid on all three legs of what is often referred to as "the conservative stool." They are deeply committed to strong national security, to social conservatism (defined by biblical morality), and to fiscal conservatism. These are the people who most fully identify with the founding principles of the American government and believe in traditional social values. The people in this group are also most likely to be religious.

Ideological Liberals

Ideological liberals, on the other hand, have a different set of priorities represented by the three-legged liberal stool. These are the people who are generally more comfortable with a more centralized governmental structure (perhaps even having a favorable view of communism or socialism), do not hold to traditional social values, and believe that free market capitalism does not promote fairness. And if these people have any association with organized religion at all, they are likely to be either uninvolved in church or to belong to a church or group which embraces theological liberalism (does not accept the Bible as authoritative). It is also not at all unusual for liberals to consider themselves Atheists or Agnostics.

The Hybridized Masses

The first step in understanding the culture war is to identify the combatant's foundational worldview authorities. In the case of the conflict between liberals and conservatives, these authorities are the tenets of Naturalism on one side and the teachings of the Bible on the other. With that knowledge in hand, we are able to examine the specific ways the beliefs of the authority sources are expressed in society.

As we examine the conflict in modern culture, it is generally the ideologues who bring the culture war to the surface. They are the ones who are most keen at recognizing opposition and defending their points of view.

That being said, the truly ideological believers are not the majority of Americans. There is another segment of the population which doesn't want to be considered ideological in this regard, on either side of the fence. The individuals in this group, no doubt, lean one way or the other, but hold values generally associated with both sides. These are people who have hybridized beliefs. Many of them are uncomfortable with the dogmatic beliefs of the ideologues and probably agree with certain points on both sides. This middle ground may include, but is not limited to, those who:

- Go to a Christian church but are socially liberal,
- Identify themselves as Christian but are pacifists,
- Consider themselves to be Christians but do not participate in church life,
- Self-identify as Christian but believe in the Theory of Evolution,
- Are socially liberal but fiscally conservative,
- Do not consider themselves religious at all, but are fiscally conservative, or
- Consider themselves liberal but are hawkish concerning military affairs.

The people in this middle group often consider themselves centrists and prefer being called political or social moderates.

In some ways, claiming the "moderate" label may seem very reasonable. After all, not being dogmatic is better, right? Why wouldn't it be better to make independent decisions based on individual situations?

The problem, though, is that a hybridized approach often involves allowing for internal inconsistencies, or even contradictions within one's beliefs. While individually choosing which policies to support is not a bad thing, it can become a problem when people make their choices based on conflicting worldview beliefs.

Worldview beliefs are, literally, exclusive. A person can't, logically, believe in God and not believe in God at the same time. One cannot believe that human beings are totally natural animals and persons created in God's image at the same time.

Just as the foundational worldview principles are exclusive, the expressions of these worldviews in daily life also fall into this category. For instance, in order to be against murder but for abortion, a person must hold contradictory beliefs. In the same way, being for free market economics yet also for equality of outcomes requires a person to hold contradictory worldview beliefs. These are just a couple of examples. We could give many other illustrations where people have these kinds of contradictory hybridized beliefs.

When people try to organize their lives using principles from contradictory worldview foundations, they will have a certain amount of internal dissidence. That being said, living with internal inconsistencies is certainly a common part of human existence. Many people manage to do this for their entire lives.

The Hybrid Lean

Though the majority of people fall into the "hybrid" category when it comes to political beliefs, there will always be a tendency to favor one side or the other. Most "middle-of-the-roaders" will self-identify as leaning one way or the other. If they don't, we can easily discover which way they lean by asking questions which reveal their beliefs.

For instance, some people consider themselves conservative because they are for conservative fiscal policies, even though they may live with someone outside of marriage (a value that is an expression of liberalism). On the other hand, a person may self-identify as a liberal because of a personal belief in abortion rights, yet also be against the legalization of marijuana (a value expression of conservatism).

The purpose in highlighting this point is simply to stress that no matter what an individual believes, the belief came from somewhere. Every belief has its root in one of the worldview camps. So, while it is fairly easy to identify liberal and conservative *beliefs* based on their origin, identifying the personal persuasion of *individuals* based on those beliefs is not nearly so cut and dried. Basically, individuals must self-identify as a conservative or liberal. However, because most people actually hold hybridized beliefs, getting to the root of an individual's overall position may prove to be somewhat difficult.

Part II
Conservative and Liberal Expressions in the Culture

While the terms "conservative" and "liberal" are primarily associated with politics, this is only one way that the more foundational worldview beliefs are actually expressed in people's lives. The truth is, these beliefs are also expressed in many other areas within a culture. This section takes the major categories of human expression and explains how liberal and conservative beliefs are concretely expressed in these other parts of life.

Chapter 6
Theology

As Lance thought about ways to help Sally better understand his conservative beliefs, an idea popped into his head. So, he took the short walk over to her office to pose the idea to her. He figured that even if she wasn't there at the moment he was not out anything.

As he walked up the hallway leading to her office, he noticed that her secretary's door was already open, so he walked in and asked if Sally was available. Sally's office door was cracked open, so when he spoke to the secretary she heard his voice and called out, "Lance, is that you? Come on in."

Lance walked over and pushed the door open. Sally sat there behind her desk with papers piled up in front of her. "Grading papers?" he asked as he walked through the doorway and pushed the door closed behind him. He then took a couple more steps and plopped himself down in the empty chair across from her.

"Yeah, no shortage of that around here. You know how that goes."

They both chuckled at that and talked a couple of minutes about the "joys" of teaching.

Then Sally asked, "What brings you over here today? This is a pleasant surprise."

Lance leaned forward a little in his chair and spoke, "Sally, I'm really enjoying this dialogue we're having. You know before this is all over I will have you converted to a good conservative."

With that, she let out a huge cackle and shot back, "Right! And there will be a massive snow storm this July in Key West, too. You know you are the one who will change your tune by the time I get through with you."

They both laughed again at that exchange, then Lance got to his point. "Listen," he said, "I just thought of a field trip we can take to help you understand my conservative point of view a little better. You up for it?"

Sally was a bit suspicious, but told him to go ahead and explain his idea.

"Okay, here's what I was thinking," Lance continued. "You know conservative beliefs in American culture are based on a Christian theistic foundation. I wanted to see if you would like to go into the belly of the beast and come to church with me in a week or two. What better way for you to do some 'field research' about what I believe?"

"Hmm, I wasn't expecting that," Sally replied. "You know I don't think much of churches. You are not trying to sneak something past me here, are you?"

"Well, Sally," Lance responded, "It would certainly make my day if you ever decided to become a Christian, but I am serious about you using this to gain some insight. In fact, I would even be willing to go with you to one of your Secular Humanist Association meetings sometime, too. I think it would be interesting."

With that concession, Sally responded, "Okay, I'll do it. And I want to go to one of your Conservative Council meetings, too – you know to see all the dumbos in action." She felt a bit smug at that last comment and chuckled to herself.

"But you do realize, there will be nothing personal about this for me. It is purely for research purposes," Sally offered as she gazed at Lance with a piercing look. "You know I don't believe in God. I think God is purely a made up concept for ignorant people who don't know how to handle life on their own."

"Well, tell me what you really think, Sally," Lance joked, as he smiled with a devilish little grin spreading across his face. He then leaned forward in his chair and said, "Listen, I know what you believe and I'm not going to get squirrely on you."

"You know, Lance," Sally offered, still using a rather stern tone, "you're a very intelligent guy. I still don't get how you can possibly believe in God, especially the way you conceive of him. I mean, you honestly believe he is a real, objective person that you can talk to. That just seems like crazy person ideas to me. You can't see him, touch him, smell him, hear him. . . ."

"Whoa, girl," Lance boomed back. "You have to remember that your belief that God does not exist is just as much a faith position as my belief that he does. You can't show any science that he doesn't exist. Beyond that, you can't account for the existence of the material universe, life or consciousness based on the science you claim your beliefs are founded upon."

"Okay, okay, I get it," Sally responded. "We'll continue this later. I'll go with you to church next Sunday. Just don't expect me to like it."

Lance laughed again and stood up to leave. Sally also stood up and reached across the desk to shake his hand. She smiled again and said, "You know I'm enjoying this conversation we are having."

****

Theology is the study of God. Some reading this may wonder why there is even a section about theology. But, as we have already seen, some belief about God is actually front and center in both conservatism and liberalism. Conservatism, in American history, is firmly planted on a theistic foundation (specifically, Christian Theism). And liberalism sits upon a naturalistic base which frames its beliefs in terms which specifically deny the existence of God.

As it turns out, though, theology is a more difficult topic to deal with than most of the other categories we will examine. That is because, in many cases, people's religious preferences seem to contradict the liberal or conservative label they claim. In particular, there are people who claim to believe in God and go to church, but who self-identify with the liberal camp. Others claim to believe in God but live their lives as if he didn't exist. On the flip side, there are those who deny the existence of God, yet don't recognize their own belief as a theological position. Understanding the theological base of the two worldview positions is an important starting point.

Conservative Theology

Conservative theology is most closely associated with Theism – belief in God. This was the default position of the founders and provided the ideas they used to establish America's major cultural institutions. Conservative beliefs are most closely tied to the Christian faith, or what is often referred to as the Judeo-Christian ethic. These beliefs get their guiding principles from the teachings of the Bible.

This approach to theology is based on the belief that God is the Creator and Sustainer of the material universe. Conservatives believe God is an objectively real person and that human beings can know him personally. They believe he revealed himself in a general way through the created order and more specifically in the Bible.

The fact that conservative theology is closely associated with the God of the Bible does not mean that the founders intended for the nation's cultural institutions to operate like a church. It also doesn't imply that society should be run as a theocracy. The public institutions were all established as secular entities. It is just that the principles which underlie the operation of the institutions are based on ideas which come out of Christian Theism. Conservatives believe that an institution can operate as a nonreligious entity but still be run based on principles which come out of a faith system.

The truth is, some underlying faith foundation forms the basis for the operation of every societal institution no matter where it is found. For example, the Bible specifically promotes the concepts of personality, holiness, justice and love. Since the institutions of American society were formed based on these notions, individualism is a key foundational concept, as is doing right and the promotion of justice and mercy. The various institutions within the society use these biblical ideals as foundational principles. They are able to operate without the institution itself actively promoting any particular religious point of view.

How Conservative Theology Is Expressed in the Culture

Conservative theology is expressed in American culture in many ways. The following are prominent examples.

1. Natural Law

The founders believed in the principle of inherent rights given by God to mankind, which exist whether or not man acknowledges them. These rights are based on principles found in the Bible. With this belief, it is natural for biblical teachings to form the basis of society's rules (laws and mores).

2. Authoritative Foundational Document

America's founders believed that the authoritative expression of God's will was found in the Bible and considered its teachings to be the ultimate source for understanding right morality. Thus, they used that model to develop an ultimate source for American law. With the writing of the constitution, they established a foundational document upon which to base all other law.

3. Freedom of Religion

Freedom of religion is founded upon the biblical concept that God created human beings to be free-will creatures. Based on this belief, the founders established, as a primary principle, that religious belief should not be forced in any respect. No one should violate any person's freedom of conscience without there being some extremely compelling health or safety reason.

4. Justice

The Bible reveals God to be completely just. Because of this belief, the founders established the biblical principle of justice as a foundational concept in the nation's legal structure. Justice, as they established it in society's institutions, demands that the government always administer the law rightly and fairly to every citizen.

5. Biblical Morality

The founders understood the God of the Bible to be holy (morally pure). They also believed that, in the Bible, God revealed not only what proper morality should look like, but also that human beings ought to conform their lives to it. As such, American law is based on biblical moral teachings. This is expressed in America's laws and social mores through such principles as the sanctity of marriage, the essential importance of truth-telling, the sanctity of life, respect for the property of others, and the like.

6. Mercy

While justice is a basic principle in biblical theology, mercy also has a place. This is based on the biblical belief that God provides mercy for the guilty if they meet particular requirements. As such, conservatives believe people ought also to forgive others and have provided specific ways to express mercy in the legal system as well as in the lives of individuals.

7. Priority of the Individual

In conservative thinking the individual holds priority over society at large. Conservatives base this approach on the biblical notion that God primarily interacts with human beings on an individual basis. They believe that God created mankind for personal fellowship with himself and also that individuals achieve eternal salvation based on an individual decision. Society exists for the individual, not the individual for society.

Continuing with this thought, the founders established a social structure which places individual responsibility above collective obligation. This does not relieve individuals of their responsibilities toward the collective. It is not a matter of the individual in opposition to society. It only indicates where the greatest priority lies.

8. Generosity of the Individual

The founders believed that God is generous with his people. Based on this character trait, they believed individuals ought, also, to take care of their fellow man. They saw this responsibility as one which should lie on the shoulders of the individual, rather than on the government.

Liberal Theology

A liberal approach to theology is most closely associated with Naturalism. In some ways, though, liberal theology is difficult to deal with because some forms seem to defy classification. Nevertheless, we can sort this out.

In its most natural form, liberal theology follows naturalistic belief – that is, it does not acknowledge the existence of any kind of supernatural reality. Its theology is expressed as some form of Atheism – the belief that God does not exist. For liberals who follow this model, all morality is relative to the situation and based on personal preference.

That being said, many who self-identify as liberals claim they do believe in God, and some are even active in Christian churches. What we generally find in these situations, however, is a Christian form which overlays a naturalistic core. This kind of theology uses religious, even Christian, vocabulary, but basically redefines the words in ways which express naturalistic concepts. The most prominent modern forms of theology in this category include liberation theology, neo-orthodoxy, existential theology, and postmodern theology.

The doctrines associated with these liberal forms of theology typically do not consider God a personal being who can be known in a personal relationship. Liberals also don't recognize the Bible as an infallible, authoritative revelation from God. On top of that, liberal theology tends to downplay the divinity of Christ and the literal reality of miracles. In general terms, this kind of theology allows individuals to create their own morality, as is consistent with Naturalism.

Liberal theology gets its core values from humanistic principles rather than biblical ones. It is very "this worldly" and without much regard for a person's eternal destiny. Interestingly, it often claims values which correspond with biblical morals, yet de-emphasizes the authority of the Bible itself as a revelation from a personal God.

Liberal theology also puts an emphasis on the collective rather than on the individual. In expressing their theology, liberals often use the term "social justice" to convey these collective values. They also generally define salvation as the saving of society, rather than the promotion of individual salvation through a personal relationship with Christ.

How Liberal Theology Is Expressed in the Culture
1. Positive Law
Liberal theology is based on naturalistic beliefs which do not recognize the existence of anything outside the material universe. Since there is no supernatural God, human beings must take responsibility for every part of life. There is no other possibility.

Using this belief foundation, the law can only be the product of human imagination. There is no notion of rights bestowed by God. Liberals believe that all rights are granted by society's leaders. Those in positions of power, then, become the ones most able to make and carry out laws.

2. No Authoritative Foundation
Since Naturalism does not recognize the existence of a God who can provide an authoritative moral law, the concept of a supreme foundational document is not a natural fit. Even if a foundational

document exists, liberals see it to be a man-made product that is subject to interpretation and change based on felt contemporary needs.

3. Freedom of Worship

In liberal belief, there is no compelling reason freedom of religion must exist. In fact, liberals generally consider freedom of religion too broad a concept because it can allow "religion" to seep into secular life.

Rather, liberals see freedom of *worship* to be a more useful idea. This allows people to exercise their religious beliefs within the framework of religious institutions and keeps them out of secular society. The purpose is to create a strict separation between church and state which allows religious expression to exist but keeps it out of any publicly governed arena.

4. Social Justice

The term "social justice" is primarily used by liberals who consider themselves religious. As such, it has become a religious term which expresses naturalistic concepts. It is the view that everyone in society deserves equal economic, political and social rights. It is a philosophy which promotes equal outcomes for everyone rather than equal opportunity. By using this term, liberals advance the notion of social salvation, as opposed to the conservative ideal of individual salvation.

5. Non-traditional Morality

Using a theology based on naturalistic beliefs, liberals don't recognize an objective or absolute basis for morality. They reject any belief which considers the possibility God might exist. For liberals, all morality is invented by human beings. Its purpose is strictly to help maintain order in society. It is relative and changeable based on what promotes survival and what is acceptable to the society at any given point in time.

6. Mercy

Humanity's highest value, using naturalistic theological concepts, is to promote survival. This conclusion comes from the belief that the material world is all that exists, so survival is the ultimate that can be accomplished. To promote survival, liberals believe society must establish rules to encourage order.

Sometimes, though, people break the rules, which is considered bad because it negatively affects society's survival possibilities. Liberals believe that the rule breakers are correctable, though, and society should give them the opportunity to adjust their behavior in order to conform to societal expectations. If rule breakers will do this, they can once again become contributors to society and help promote survival. Those who follow through justify the mercy they receive.

As liberals see humans as purely physical beings, they believe rule breaking is due to some kind of abnormality – related either to a person's physical or social situation. The remedy, then, is to somehow correct these defects. When meting out justice, the authorities are justified in taking into account mitigating factors if the rule breaker is able to show that he or she can learn to conform to society's expectations. This principle applies at the personal level as well as within the legal system.

7. Priority of the Collective

For liberals, the highest possible value is survival of the species. That belief is primary because, for them, the material universe is all that exists. With this starting point, they consider survival is best accomplished through collective, as opposed to individual, action. Thus, the needs of the collective take priority over the needs and wants of the individual. Those in leadership positions are generally the ones who determine how that is expressed in the culture.

8. Generosity of the Collective

Since the survival of the collective is the highest priority in liberal theology, it becomes the responsibility of the entire society to make sure they take care of all members. The most effective way to express this is to distribute society's goods and services in a way which assure equal outcomes. The governing authorities do this by taxing the higher producers and redistributing it to those with less.

Chapter 7
Philosophy

"Okay, I will say it. It was an interesting time with you at church," Sally admitted, as she and Lance sat eating at the diner the following Thursday. "Not that I believe any of that God dribble or anything, but the people were nice and it was interesting to get a bit more insight on the perspective of people who agree with you."

"Well, I'm glad you had a good experience," Lance replied as he started digging into his burger and fries. "They are really good folks and, as I hope you saw, they are not just a bunch of hayseeds. There are a number of them who are members of the conservative forum, you know."

After talking about the church experience for a while, Sally zeroed in on one of the main things she still had a difficult time swallowing. "Listen, Lance, here is what I have a hard time getting. How is it possible for you to actually believe that there is an objectively real spiritual realm? It goes against everything we know based on science."

"So now you are turning your attention to philosophy, are you?" Lance asked as he downed another fry. "The nature of reality and values. Very interesting topic, indeed. So, you struggle to understand how I can bring myself to believe in God since there is no science to support it. At the same time, you don't see any difficulty believing, without any science to back it up, that all of the various aspects of reality came into being by naturalistic evolutionary processes. Is that what you are saying?"

Sally didn't immediately answer Lance on that one. She just sat there for a few moments and thought about it. "You know," she finally replied, "that is one of the issues that is sometimes troubling. There are things that scientists aren't able to understand yet using the scientific method, though I do believe that in the future science will come up with how it all happens."

"Sally, Sally, Sally," Lance shot back shaking his head. "Don't you realize the faith nature of what you have just said? Yet you insist that in spite of everything, there is a naturalistic explanation for it all. How do you know that what you are saying is true?"

Sally didn't waste any time answering back this time. "It just can't be any other way. There is no other possibility. If God doesn't exist, and I don't believe he does, then naturalistic answers are the only possibility."

"Sally, even your answer betrays a problem." Lance countered. "You said, 'IF God doesn't exist.' You said, you 'BELIEVE' that he doesn't. Those are not scientific answers. They are all based on faith."

"You just don't understand the nature of science," Sally retorted. "There are many things science has not yet solved which must be further explored to get to the final answers. That doesn't mean we believe by faith. It means that we are waiting for science to catch up."

"That is assuming it is possible for it to catch up. And that assumes that there is no such thing as a supernatural reality. Looks to me like there is a whole lot of 'assumin' going on," Lance answered back. "See, this is where our worldviews clash philosophically. I BELIEVE there is such a thing as a supernatural reality. As such I believe that there is a part of the human person that cannot be accessed by naturalistic methodology. That is how I understand reality. So, to get to the bottom of the nature of humanity, I believe that you have to go after evidence which is not all natural. Sure, there is a natural part of humanity that can be understood using science. But some evidence has to be accessed by logic and other based on human experience. You, on the other hand, BELIEVE everything has a natural explanation that can ultimately be accessed by science. Those are two entirely different sets of beliefs that operate off of entirely different worldview foundations."

"I understand what you are saying, Lance," Sally replied as she settled in against the seat back. "And it is a dilemma, isn't it? I can't bring myself to believe what you believe and you can't believe what I believe. So how can we ever resolve this?"

"Oh, I've got that figured out," said Lance as he chuckled out loud. "All you have to do is just abandon your naturalistic foolishness and start believing in God."

At that, Sally burst out laughing. "Yeah, fat chance on that one," she shot back as she signaled the waiter. "I simply can't believe what doesn't ring true."

At that, the waiter came up and give them their bills and began clearing the table. Sally and Lance got up and headed toward the cashier. While they were waiting to pay, Sally looked at Lance and said, "Shall we pick it up again next week?"

"I'm game," Lance replied back. "I'm enjoying getting the best of you."

Sally laughed again. "The day you get the best of me will be the day our football team gets beat by the city pee-wees. Listen, you have a great one. See you next week."

"Great, see you then," Lance replied.

****

Philosophy is the study of reality, knowledge and values. It investigates these three topics by examining their nature, causes and principles. People who study philosophy must use logical reasoning rather than scientific methods. Although some people like to think that everything can ultimately be known using scientific inquiry, that is simply not possible. There are many things human beings deal with which science simply has no way to investigate. In fact, scientific investigation, itself, is built upon a philosophical foundation.

To even contemplate philosophy, there must be a being who is capable of self-conscious thought. Nonhuman creatures cannot do that. Only humans have that capability. People's beliefs about the nature of humanity (one of the three essential worldview questions) will determine how they contemplate philosophy.

Conservative Philosophy

Conservative philosophy in America is based on the beliefs of Christian Theism. It is founded upon a type of dualism where both body (the physical part of a person) and mind (the spiritual part of a person) are believed to be objectively real. With a belief in this kind of dualism, it is possible to combine both faith and reason into the consideration of reality, knowledge and values.

Philosophy which is based on a theistic foundation takes seriously the existence of both physical and spiritual reality. Thus, conservatives understand the body to be a system which operates based on natural laws. They also believe in a supernatural existence and that the human mind is capable of operating beyond the natural world. In other words, the mind is not physical. It is the part of the human person that connects the body (using the physical brain) and the spirit. The logical conclusion, based on this particular kind of dualism, is that human beings are able to personally interact with other spiritual beings, both human and supernatural.

Conservative philosophy is founded squarely upon the belief that mind (a being capable of thought) came before matter (the natural universe). Conservatives believe that the particular mind which existed before matter is the God of the Bible. He, then, is the one responsible for creating matter (the material universe). Assuming this is true, human beings can only understand the true nature of reality, knowledge and values when God reveals them. That revelation is found in the Bible. Using that foundation, let's explore what the Bible teaches about the nature of reality, knowledge and values.

Reality

Conservative philosophy believes that both God and the material universe are factually real. Conservatives believe God exists as an objectively real person. They also believe that material reality did not exist until God created it. When he did create it, he made it to operate according to natural laws. In fact, God established natural laws to maintain the operation of his creation.

Also, as Creator, God is capable of interacting with his creation in ways which do not disturb its natural operation. Thus, he is able to communicate with human beings who live within the confines of his material creation.

Knowledge

Conservatives also believe God is the ultimate source of knowledge. He is a being whose very existence includes the ability to know. The reason human beings have this ability is that we are created in the image of God. In mankind, God created a being who has many of the personhood characteristics that exist within himself.

One of these characteristics is the capacity for knowledge. As a result, the knowledge that exists in humans has its origin outside the natural universe. There are two elements of this knowledge that man is able to tap into.

The first is the ability to learn things about the natural universe we inhabit. This not only includes the material elements of the universe, which is the domain of science, but also elements which exist beyond scientific inquiry – the laws of logic and matters related to mind and spirit. Since conservatives also understand these to be objectively real parts of God's creation, the ability to study and understand them are included in the use of knowledge.

The second aspect of knowledge comes from outside the natural abilities of humans. Conservatives believe that God gave a special revelation to mankind from beyond the physical universe as a means of imparting knowledge of eternal/spiritual matters.

We are able to understand the concept of knowledge because of how God ordered reality. It can be expressed as:

- mind existed before matter,
- God existed before humanity,
- design existed before creation,
- life emerged from life,
- enlightenment (human understanding) emerged from light (God's revelation), and
- all elements of reality reflect order.

Conservative philosophy also believes that the mind is separate from the physical body. Our thinking process uses functions which operate outside of the natural world. Certainly the mind operates on and influences the body and vice versa, but they are not the same thing. Matter (the brain) exists, something other than matter (mind) exists, and they interact with each other. Consciousness is a mental (spiritual) concept, not a physical one.

Values

Conservative philosophy also believes that values come from an eternal source. And, as was true with reality and knowledge above, values exist concretely. In fact, conservatives believe that true values come from the character of God himself. Truth, love, righteousness, and justice are the foundation stones of conservative values because they are expressions of the person of God.

Since God exists outside the material universe, human knowledge of his values is dependent upon special revelation. And, since God exists beyond man's unaided reason, he had to purposefully share knowledge of these values with humanity in human language or there would be no way of knowing them. The revelation that God gave of himself in the Bible expresses his personhood characteristics as values which humanity should understand and incorporate into life.

How Conservative Philosophy Is Expressed in the Culture
Reality

Since conservatives believe God actually exists, allowing religious beliefs to have an influence in the public sector is merely a recognition of reality. This does not mean that it is acceptable for the government to promote any particular religion. It does, however, allow for individuals to express their faith in what they do in public. Expressions of this might be seen in such things as allowing public religious expressions at Christmas, permitting religious symbols on public monuments, granting the right to pray at public meetings, allowing the posting of the 10 Commandments on courthouse walls, and the like.

At the same time, conservatives also see the material world as objectively real and operating based on natural laws. As such, they take science seriously and don't see a conflict between the spiritual and the material.

Knowledge

Conservatives understand humans to be essentially spiritual beings who exist in a physical body. As such, knowledge exists as an element of both the material and the spiritual realms. They believe that knowledge can be used in the material world but can also operate beyond it as God reveals his will and his ways. For conservatives, knowledge is about more than mere facts, but also includes the ability to discern information from spiritual sources. Because of this, conservatives believe academic study should not be limited only to naturalistic worldview approaches.

Values

Since conservatives recognize God to be a person who has revealed himself and his ways in the Bible, conservative values are the same as biblical values. As such, laws, and all other expressions of morality within society, are built upon the values expressed in the Bible. Non-biblical values are, thus, considered immoral.

Liberal Philosophy

Liberal philosophy is based on the beliefs of Naturalism. It is expressed as a type of monism where all of reality exists strictly within the framework of the physical universe. Liberals believe that the work of the mind is nothing more than the operation of the physical brain. Thus, what people sometimes sense as the ability of the mind to reach beyond the body is actually not that at all. They believe that kind of perception only occurs because the physical human brain has evolved to a high enough level of complexity to allow for self-conscious thought. To them, religious faith is nothing more than an illusion. Liberals believe that science can, or will soon be able to, account for all thought processes based on the natural operation of the brain.

Liberal philosophy is founded upon the idea that matter came first and mind evolved out of it as naturalistic evolution ran its course. As such, only creatures whose brains have evolved the capacity to think self-consciously (human beings) are able to deal with the topics of reality, knowledge and values.

Reality

Based on its naturalistic presuppositions, liberal philosophy only considers the material universe to be objectively real. There is nothing outside it. Liberals believe that everything in all of reality operates according to natural laws.

Knowledge

The origin of knowledge, based on liberal philosophy, comes from the evolutionary development of the human brain. Liberals believe that the human brain has evolved to a high enough level of complexity for self-conscious thought to occur. As a result, the knowledge that humans are able to acquire has its origin in the brain's evolutionary development. They believe the brain is essentially a biological computer. Knowledge becomes possible as bits of information are stored and accessed based on biological, electrical and chemical functions within the brain.

Liberals understand the concept of knowledge through a completely natural paradigm. The way this is expressed is that:

- matter existed before mind,
- humans evolved to their current state from less complex life forms,
- design evolved out of chaos,
- life emerged from non-life,
- enlightenment (human understanding) emerged as an evolutionary product of brain development, and
- all elements of reality emerged from chaos.

Values

Based on liberal philosophy, values are founded upon naturalistic presuppositions. Liberals believe that human beings create values based on the needs of the individual and of social groups. There is no God to reveal values from beyond the material universe, so human beings must develop all values themselves. Typically, liberals believe humans develop values as a survival mechanism as a part of the evolutionary process. They choose appropriate values for their social groups based on what they perceive will give them the best chance of survival.

How Liberal Philosophy Is Expressed in the Culture
Reality

Since liberals do not believe that an eternal mind exists beyond the material universe, a liberal understanding of reality must be based purely on human reason. As such, any ideas which include belief in God are considered superstitious and unreal. This is expressed in the culture as a resistance to any kind of spiritual expression. Things that are quite acceptable to conservatives (allowing public religious expressions at Christmas, religious symbols on public monuments, the posting of the 10 Commandments on courthouse walls, and the like) are viewed by liberals as misguided and unacceptable.

Knowledge

Liberals believe human beings are purely physical creatures. As such, they believe knowledge exists only because of the operation of the human brain. In the culture, they reject any non-naturalistic approach to dealing with academic study and do not set any limits, based on moral reasoning, on how knowledge can be used.

Values

Liberals believe that all values are derived from human reason, with survival being the ultimate goal. As such, they believe all laws, and every other expression of morality within a society, are purely functional items. They do not believe there is any such thing as objectively real moral or immoral acts. Matters are considered wrong and bad if they work against the survival of the community. Anything beyond that is potentially acceptable.

Chapter 8
Anthropology

"Hey Sally. Gorgeous day, isn't it?" Lance called out. "I hate to go in the diner with it nice like this outside."

It was Thursday again. This time Lance and Sally ran into each other just down the street as they were walking to meet each other for their weekly "conversation" at the diner.

"I agree completely," Sally replied back. "What say we order our food for carry out and go over to a picnic table in the park across the street?"

Lance nodded approvingly. "Let's do it."

At that, they went in, ordered their food and took it over to the park. As they sat down at an empty picnic table, they noticed a whole group of elementary aged kids playing on the playground equipment nearby. Their teachers were standing around the perimeter keeping a close eye on them all.

"It's so much fun to watch the kids enjoying themselves like that. I remember those days. I always liked the swing set best," Sally said nostalgically. "I would spend hours swinging back and forth with the wind blowing in my face. Sometimes I wish I could go back to those days of innocence."

"Yeah, those were good times, weren't they," Lance agreed. "I liked the merry-go-round, myself."

"Notice how there are three distinct ethnic groups among the kids. See that?" Sally remarked as she carefully observed their interaction.

"That would certainly be something Sally would pick up on," Lance thought to himself.

"Sally," Lance spoke up, "from your perspective, what do you see there?"

"Okay," Sally observed. "Look at the group on the right playing in the sand. They are almost all Asian. The group on the swings are mostly African-American. And you see over there on the hopscotch court, those kids are mostly white."

As Sally pointed this out, Lance saw that her observations were right. Actually, all three groups also contained kids of other ethnicities, but in general she was spot on.

"So what do you make of that?" Lance asked. "Why do you consider that important?"

"Haven't you ever studied anthropology?" Sally asked. "Anthropological studies suggest that each of the groups have their own distinct cultural backgrounds. Those different backgrounds predispose the kids to enjoy different kinds of activities."

"Well, Sally, how do you know it is the cultural differences that account for that?" Lance responded. "Maybe they decided what to play based on individual preferences, or just to be with a friend, rather than on cultural predispositions. How do you know that is not true?"

"Think about it, Lance. Why do you suppose the individuals make their particular choices?" Sally tried to sum up her entire worldview in this single argument. "It is because they are culturally predisposed to it."

"But Sally," Lance countered, "I remember when I was a kid their age. I played different games at different times. One day I would play hopscotch, another day tether ball, another day I would swing. And, as I recall, the other kids did the same thing. I don't think it has anything to do with a cultural predisposition."

"We're back to the same issue we ran into before, aren't we, Lance?" Sally countered. "You are arguing for a point of view that puts a priority on some kind of spiritual independence for individuals while I am arguing for the influence of naturalistic evolution."

At that, Lance nodded in agreement. "Yes, it seems that we keep coming back to that difference."

They continued discussing that topic for a while until they finished eating. At that point it was time for them to head back to their offices. As they got up to leave, Sally spoke up. "Hey Lance, I went to your church meeting a few weeks ago, now it is payback time. Our Humanist Association meets next Tuesday evening. How about coming. In fact, I have an idea if you don't mind being put on the spot."

"Oh my, what have you got up your sleeve?" Lance asked. He could just see her putting him in an embarrassing situation. "Are you planning on throwing me to the wolves? You know I didn't do that to you."

"No, nothing like that. Well, not exactly, anyway," Sally replied as she tried to soften the impact. "Next week we are going to have a panel discussion on the nature of society. I thought it might be interesting to have your theistic perspective as a part of the discussion. It would spice things up a little."

"I don't know, Sally. Is it going to be twenty against one with people pounding me to death?"

"No, Lance, nothing like that" Sally responded. "They will be very respectful. Actually, over the last several weeks I have been sharing with some of them about our conversations and it has piqued their interest. I believe they will be very interested to hear you directly."

"Okay, I will do it," Lance offered. "But I would appreciate one thing."

"What's that?" Sally asked.

Lance replied, "Before next week, I want a little more detail about the discussion – the discussion questions or whatever."

"Fair enough. I will get that to you tomorrow. I'll e-mail you. Hey, and thanks for your willingness to do it. Seriously, I am really excited that the others are going to get to interact with someone from the other side that is not a hayseed," Sally teased as she set out on her way.

"Yeah, I love you, too," Lance retorted. "See you next week."

****

The word anthropology means the study of man. This field of study overlaps considerably with sociology, humanities and biology. That said, anthropology does have its own unique focus. It is a social science which is concerned primarily with human culture, as well as the physical and social characteristics that create a culture. Often the focus of anthropology is to compare one group of humans to another, or even human groups with animal groups. To do this, anthropologists concentrate primarily on social institutions, religion, art, history, mythology, and common mores.

Conservative Anthropology

Conservative anthropology is based on the beliefs of Christian Theism. It begins with the notion that God created man in his own image. As such, conservatives not only consider man a physical creature they can study using scientific methods, but also a spiritual being with characteristics which go beyond the physical.

Since humans are physical creatures that express themselves in the physical world, conservatives believe scientists can examine and evaluate the various elements of culture in different places throughout the world. In doing this, they are able to learn more about the nature of the physical life of human beings.

But as humans are also spiritual creatures, conservative anthropologists must consider something beyond the physical. Human beings also use their spiritual capabilities (free will, creativity, knowledge, self-consciousness, etc.) to express their lives in the physical world. Thus, conservatives believe that studying the outward expressions of these abilities can give additional insight into human nature.

The Nature of Human Beings
Spiritual

Conservative anthropology views human beings as essentially spiritual creatures who exist in a physical body. This approach is based on the belief that God, who is an objectively real person, created mankind in his own image. This is expressed in humans through characteristics which go beyond mere physical attributes – characteristics such as creativity, self-consciousness, free will, the ability to think abstractly and the like. These attributes cannot be studied directly, but can be indirectly observed as they are expressed in human life.

Biological

While recognizing humans to be essentially spiritual creatures, conservatives also recognize that they are physical beings. As such, there are elements of human life and culture which can be studied using the scientific method.

Social

Conservative anthropology also recognizes that human beings are social creatures. Humans express this social element as they group themselves into communities, each with its own unique cultural characteristics. While conservatives recognize that the source of culture emerges out of people's spiritual nature which science cannot directly study, they also believe there is a part which they can observe and analyze based on scientific methodology.

It is important to note that while conservatives consider the social aspect of humanity to be significant, the most important focus is on the individual. The belief that God purposefully created man in his own image forms the foundation of this notion.

The Nature of Human Culture

Conservative anthropology looks at human culture and sees it made up of spiritual beings who are housed in physical bodies. Conservatives believe human creatures express their spiritual characteristics in the material world. There are many areas where this is seen.

Religion

Conservative anthropology bases its understanding of religion on the teachings of the Bible. The biblical teaching is that God created mankind and revealed himself directly to the first humans. The humans then passed on this knowledge about God from generation to generation.

But in the process of passing it down, many cultures distorted it. This distortion accounts for the various worldviews and belief systems in existence. Over time, in order to insure the truth remained, God revealed himself through the nation of Israel and through Jesus Christ. Conservatives believe that all other religious beliefs must be measured against what is taught in the Bible.

The Arts and Entertainment

Human beings express their personhood through various art forms. The forms include painting, music, sculpture, theater, and the like. Conservatives see human ability to express themselves creatively to be an outward expression of the belief that God made man in his own image.

History and Mythology

Conservative anthropology recognizes that there is an overarching meaning in history. This meaning emerges from God's purpose in the Creation. It assumes that the human story is an expression of how people groups, through the ages, have interpreted that purpose in their cultures. The very fact that a culture's history is passed down through the ages, via oral or written traditions, is evidence that humans recognize the significance of historical events as they play out in time.

Ethics and Morality

Based on conservative beliefs, God has revealed himself to humanity. Conservatives believe he not only did this through the Bible, but also in the human conscience. As such, they consider that human beings have an innate understanding of basic morality which has a personal eternal source. This includes a sense of fairness, justice, proper sexual behavior, and an appreciation for life.

How Conservative Anthropology is Expressed in Culture
Religion

As conservative anthropology is built upon the beliefs of Christian Theism, conservatives view religion in very concrete terms. They understand God to be an objectively real person who revealed himself to mankind in the Bible. As such, they do not view religious faith merely as a form to practice, but as objective truth to engage. As the nation's founders recognized and believed this to be true, they made the principles of the Christian religion an integral part of American culture from its beginning.

Art and Entertainment

As conservative belief is based on biblical morality, conservatives measure the standards for and appropriateness of art and entertainment by the teachings of the Bible. In general terms, they view the various expressions of art and entertainment as good things because they allow human beings to express an element of God's image in their lives. That being said, they also believe there are moral lines which should not be crossed when creating art and entertainment. As an expression of this, they draw moral lines in law and in social mores to clarify what is acceptable and what is not.

History and Mythology

Conservatives recognize history as meaningful based on God's purposes for creating the world. Since history has meaning, conservatives look at and evaluate the flow of history, and historical events, in light of what God has revealed in the Bible as his will.

This viewpoint also informs the way conservatives teach history in schools. They recognize the existence of absolute truth and teach history based on the belief that the Bible reveals the nature of that truth. With this filter in place, it is also possible to judge historical events based on biblical morality.

Ethics and Morality

Conservatives believe in the existence of an objective right and wrong based on God's revelation in the Bible. As such, they seek to direct the actions of individuals and society in ways which conform to biblical truth. This is expressed in culture as society creates laws, folkways and mores based on biblical morality.

Liberal Anthropology

Liberal anthropology is based on the presuppositions of Naturalism. It does not acknowledge the existence of God or any supernatural reality. As such, liberals conduct anthropological studies based on the belief that human beings are merely one species of natural animal among many on earth. The entire purpose of anthropology, then, is to gain a holistic understanding of the human animal and of human nature using the tools of modern science. Liberal anthropologists generally do this by attempting to analyze the biological, linguistic, historic and cultural aspects of humanity based strictly on naturalistic assumptions. To do this they study man using naturalistic biology, genetics, archeology, and linguistics, as well as direct observation of societies in their natural environments.

The Nature of Human Beings
Biological

Liberal anthropology understands human beings to be strictly biological creatures. Liberals evaluate every aspect of individual human life and social expression on the principles of naturalistic evolution. They believe that, by chance, human beings are the animal species which evolved a complex enough brain to become self-aware.

They do not believe in a God who could reveal proper morality, so the human animal must base all its actions on what it considers best for any given situation.

Social

Liberal anthropology believes human social organization is the natural evolutionary expression of humanity's quest for survival. Liberals consider that living in social groupings enhances the survivability of the species. For that reason, humans naturally form groups which develop their own unique cultural expressions.

The Nature of Human Culture
Religion

Liberal anthropology, since it is based on Naturalism, does not recognize the existence of God or any supernatural reality. As such, liberals view religion strictly as a material cultural institution designed to help organize a society. When evaluating a culture's religious expressions, liberals merely try to understand what part religion plays in the functioning of the society. They base their evaluations purely on the part religion plays in the material culture, with no consideration that there may be some actual spiritual element at play.

Art and Entertainment

Liberal anthropology evaluates art and entertainment completely on naturalistic worldview principles. Liberals see human beings as nothing more than natural animals with highly evolved brains. Thus, the development of art and entertainment do nothing more than help explain how that high level brain development is used to develop the culture.

History and Mythology

Liberal anthropology recognizes no overarching meaning in history. As such, the human story is nothing more than a record of the thoughts and actions of those who came before. Liberals do not recognize any meaning associated with human history beyond what they can learn about the people they investigate or what they can do to use it for their own ends.

Ethics and Morality

Based on liberal beliefs, God does not exist so there can be no such thing as an objectively real morality. Liberals believe the ethics and morality developed within any given culture is based entirely on function – what best promotes the survival of the culture.

How Liberal Anthropology is Expressed in Culture
Religion

As liberal anthropology is founded upon naturalistic beliefs, liberals view religion in completely relative and material terms. They don't recognize the existence of any kind of supernatural reality. As such, they see religious faith purely as a form to practice without any objective basis in reality. They believe people express the forms in the culture using religious organizations and rituals. Liberals believe that these are purely material social forms which promote the survival of the society, even though the people practicing them believe there is an actual spiritual element to them.

Art and Entertainment

Liberal belief is based completely on a relativistic understanding of morality. Thus, liberals believe cultures determine the standards for and appropriateness of art and entertainment based completely on human preference. Liberals view expressions of art and entertainment as good or bad according to personal and corporate evaluations, not on anything innately good or bad in the art or entertainment itself. The only restrictions they consider acceptable are matters society believes might cause harm to the culture.

History and Mythology

Liberals do not recognize that history has any innate meaning at all. That is because, for meaning to exist, there must be some person overseeing history who is able to assign meaning to it. Liberals don't believe such a creature exists.

Since history has no innate meaning, liberals look at and evaluate the flow of history, as well as individual historical events, purely as a record of the past. This is reflected in the way they teach history in schools. Liberal historians can make no objective moral evaluation of any historical event. They can only make moral judgments based on individual opinion. Objectively speaking, history is nothing more than a record of past events.

Ethics and Morality

Liberals believe there is no such thing as an objective right and wrong. They must base all moral allowances and restrictions purely on how a culture's leaders believe they affect the development and survival of the culture. Liberals seek to direct the actions of individuals, and of society, in ways which conform to the preferences of the masses or of the leaders who have the power to influence it.

Chapter 9
Sociology

As agreed, Lance met Sally outside of the meeting hall about twenty minutes early. She wanted time to introduce him around before they got going.

"Hey, Lance," Sally called out from her car as she stepped out and headed toward him. "How are you doing?"

"I'm great! So this is the lion's den?" Lance called back as he chuckled out loud.

Sally laughed, too, at his comment. That is one thing she really liked about Lance, he had a great sense of humor and was a good sport. "Shall we go in?" she asked.

Lance thrust his arm in the air in a "first down" motion and replied, "I'm with you."

As they entered the front door, it was evident that people were already at work setting up for the meeting. There were several putting out chairs while another group set up the table for the panel discussion. Over in the corner, another group was setting up some refreshments.

For the next few minutes, Sally took Lance around and made the introductions. Everyone seemed genuinely glad to see him and were very complimentary because of what Sally had shared about their conversations. Lance even saw a few colleagues from the university that he knew.

Sally was the president of the association this year, so when it was time she called the meeting to order and took care of the preliminaries. As Lance looked around, he counted about forty people – actually a pretty good representation for a meeting like this. He wondered if they had come hoping to see the slaughter of the lamb. At this thought, he chuckled to himself.

A few minutes later, Sally announced that it was time for the panel discussion and called four people to the front. On the panel was a planner from the city planning department, Bill Johnson, Dr.

Jack Ormond, a zoologist from the local zoo, a sociology professor from the university, Dr. Janice Crosby, and Lance. It so happened that Lance knew Janice from the school. They had been on several academic committees together.

Sally then introduced the topic to get things started. She began, "Today's topic is a symposium on the nature of society. Bill Johnson will be talking about how the city uses sociological information to plan for the city's growth. Jack Ormond will give us some insight on the differences and similarities between the societies that humans form and those of other animal species. Dr. Janice Crosby and Dr. Lance Jackson will be dealing with the more philosophical aspects of the nature of society. Of course, Dr. Crosby is one of our own and will be speaking from the point of view that human society is the result of the evolutionary development of the human species. Dr. Jackson is a Theist and believes that human beings are specially created by God and, thus, that the nature of society reflects the work of God in the world. Please make them all feel welcome."

After the introductions, each of the four took turns laying out their points of view. Then, after the short presentations, the floor was opened up for questions. The meeting went on for just over an hour, then Sally stood up and closed it out.

Following the panel, everybody just hung around, enjoyed the refreshments and talked. In this setting, everyone was especially intrigued with Lance and engaged him energetically in conversation.

After they were done, Sally and Lance walked out to the parking lot together. "Well," Sally asked, "What did you think? Were they too hard on you?"

"Actually," Lance replied, "I enjoyed it. Everyone was very respectful. I did feel a bit under the microscope, but it was a good experience. So, did I come across as a hayseed?" Lance laughed out loud.

Sally couldn't help but join him in the laughter. "No! You came across as the intelligent, though misguided, guy that you are," Sally retorted. "I really do appreciate you doing it, and for being such a good sport."

"My pleasure," Lance replied. "See you at the diner again next week?"

"Sounds good to me," Sally answered back.

At that, they both got into their cars and drove off. It had been a very interesting evening, indeed.

****

Sociology is the study of human social behavior. It is particularly focused on the origins, organization, institutions, and development of human society. As with every other topic we have looked at, liberals and conservatives have entirely different ways of thinking about these issues based on their worldview foundations.

Conservative Sociology

While conservative sociology is interested, to a degree, in all of the institutions found in society, three are especially emphasized because of the attention they receive in the Bible. The three are: traditional family, church and state.

Conservative sociology begins with the Theistic assumption that God created the world. Conservatives believe that, in the Bible, God gave instructions to humanity regarding how they should order society based on his purposes. They believe there is a way society ought to be ordered and it is up to the members of society to try and order it that way.

Conservatives also believe that human nature plays an important part in society's structure. Conservative belief assumes that God created human beings in his image but that they now exist in a fallen condition. Based on that assumption, conservatives believe society is also naturally flawed.

At the same time, they believe there is an ideal toward which humans should strive. That ideal corresponds with God's purpose for his created order as revealed in the Bible. In other words, God created man to operate within a social framework for the purpose of accomplishing his work in the world.

The Individual and Society

Conservative sociology affirms that society is very important. That being said, the value of the individual is considered to be higher than society at large. It is individuals who are responsible before God for how society operates.

An important element of the human person, which affects the development of society, is human free will. Conservative sociology affirms that individuals have an actual free will and are responsible before God for the choices they make as they live life. Humans are capable of choosing between varying alternatives, and those choices shape society.

Based on the Fall, as it is explained in the Bible, conservatives also believe that individuals have an internal tendency toward doing evil acts and are guilty before God for their bad choices. This tendency in individuals also causes society to lean in that direction. As such, humans are responsible before God when societal degradation happens.

As a result, conservative sociology tries to understand society in light of human free-will choices and the consequences of those choices. Wrong choices result in individual alienation from God which leads to bad results in the social order.

In spite of the fact that man tends toward evil, conservative sociology has an optimistic view because it understands that God grants grace. Conservatives believe it is possible to overcome negative human tendencies to the degree people follow God and turn society toward him.

Even though conservative sociology places a higher value on the individual than on society, conservatives still believe the social order is vitally important. They consider that God created human beings in his image which makes them social beings. This plays out in the world as humans form themselves into social units. As such, society also has a role to play in the development of individuals and in the purposes of God.

Conservatives believe humans are creatures which God intentionally created as relational beings. Because of a fallen human nature, though, they continually fail at relationships on an individual level. This individual failure also affects the development of society. With this in mind, sociologists are able to recognize and understand the value of both individuals and society, and to keep things in their proper perspective.

Primary Societal Institutions

As was noted earlier, there are three institutions that are of special interest to conservatives – family, church, and state. These three are particularly prescribed in the Bible.

Conservatives believe God ordained the family to be the most foundational institution in society. They affirm that the core of a family unit consists of a man and woman who are married and committed to one another for life. This is the place where children can be brought into the world and nurtured most effectively. The family is the social unit which determines the health of a society at its most fundamental level. Lifestyles a society accepts which operate outside this boundary end up degrading and destroying it.

A second foundational institution in society is the church. It is called on to be society's moral backbone. It is the institution which focuses primarily on understanding the fallen nature of humanity and on calling people to follow God and his purposes.

The third foundational institution is the state. The primary function of the state is to maintain order and promote justice in society. For human beings to function effectively in the world, there must be order and justice. The state is the institution charged with maintaining these functions.

While the three institutions above are primary, society is composed of numerous other institutions which are also important to its operation. These include such institutions as education, news media, entertainment, medicine, agriculture, law enforcement, business entities and the like. For conservatives, all of these are important and are influenced by the decisions individuals make as they live in society.

How Conservative Sociology is Expressed in the Culture
Family

In conservative sociology, marriage is the bedrock foundation of society. As goes marriage, so goes the society. Conservatives understand marriage to exist based strictly on a biblical foundation – one man and one woman for life. The purpose of the marriage relationship is to provide an environment where individuals can most effectively grow and develop. It is the place where spouses can fulfill their highest potential and children can find safety and nurture. When family is established based on this model, society will thrive. When the model is broken down by divorce, alternative understandings of marriage, and sexual relationships outside of marriage, not only does it break down the family, but society at large. As such, conservatives place a strong emphasis on traditional marriage and biblical morality regarding sexual relationships.

Church

Conservative sociology begins with belief in the God of the Bible. As such, conservatives believe faith in and worship of him is an important key to keeping society strong and stable. They believe that participation in church serves as a key element of society to promote social interaction and an understanding of God and his purposes. They believe that, ideally, all members of society should actively participate in this institution.

Government

Government is another of the key institutions of society based on conservative sociology. Government should not, however, have priority over the individual. Its proper place is to serve the individual. The American government was specifically set up to operate in this way with checks and balances to make sure it did not infringe the rights of individual citizens. Conservatives seek to keep the government in check by limiting its power and creating mechanisms which make it difficult for the government to overstep its bounds.

That being said, government has a very specific and important role to play. That role is to maintain order and promote justice for all citizens. Order is critical because an orderly environment is necessary to provide a stable place for families to thrive and for citizens to do productive work – including the work of God. Justice is critical because it allows for all individuals to live safely and productively within society.

Education

Education, in the context of conservative sociology, is based on a Theistic understanding of reality and has a high priority. The basis for education is found in the belief that God created man in his own image with the capacity for knowledge. God has also revealed that human beings should be diligent in developing excellence in every part of life. To accomplish these things, conservatives place a strong emphasis on education.

Conservatives also believe in the existence of objective truth. As such, an important aspect of education is to pass truth to the next generation. This includes the truth that is revealed by God in the Bible.

News Media

Conservative sociology understands that communication within a societal structure is important. As such, the news media serves an important function within the structure. In conservative thinking, the key principle for delivering news is truth. Conservatives have no problem with people delivering commentary, but news should always be focused on promoting truth.

Entertainment

Entertainment is also an important element in conservative sociology, but should be enjoyed based on biblical notions of morality. Much entertainment in modern culture is based on a view of morality which has no such constraints. Conservatives believe this kind of disregard for biblical morality degrades society and leads people away from God.

Medicine

Conservative sociology begins with the notion that man is a fallen creature. This fallenness not only includes the tendency to sin, but also involves the brokenness in the physical universe itself. It was not God's intention for sickness and disease to be a part of his creation, and he did not create it that way. Since it does exist, however, conservatives believe it is good and appropriate to do everything possible to overcome its effects. Since the world operates based on natural laws, scientists are able to understand the human body and develop medical remedies.

Agriculture

Based on biblical principles regarding economics, conservative sociology looks at agriculture as an institution which should be governed by the free market. Those who work should eat and those not willing to work should not be rewarded. In cases where people have particular problems taking care of themselves, the community is charged with helping them voluntarily.

Law Enforcement

One important function of government, based on conservative beliefs, is to promote order. Conservative sociology sees law enforcement as a key institution for handling this duty. While enforcing the law, however, conservatives believe law enforcement officials are to do their work in such a way as to also promote justice.

Businesses/Corporations

Since conservative sociology is based on the priority of the individual, rather than of the collective, individuals should approach work using concepts and methodologies which promote the advancement of the individual. And, as conservatives believe biblical morality is the proper basis of life, people should carry out business in a way which reflects honesty and integrity, and provides the best opportunity for individuals to achieve their highest potential.

Liberal Sociology

Liberal sociology is founded upon the naturalistic worldview assumption that there is no such thing as a supernatural reality. As such, mankind does not exist for any objective purpose. Humans are merely animal creatures which have evolved from mindless matter and will live life until they meet physical death. Liberals believe that this evolutionary process developed in a way which caused human beings to be social animals as a means of survival. Since there is no overarching purpose for humankind, there is also, by extension, no purpose for society other than survival. Additionally, without a God to provide direction, there is no objective guidance for how society ought to be formed. A society can legitimately become whatever its citizens decide is appropriate.

The Individual and Society

Based on naturalistic concepts, liberal sociology believes that society is more important than the individual. The reason for this is that survival requires the interactive cooperation of its members. Liberals believe that survival is much easier when society is organized effectively, and very difficult if individuals try to make it on their own.

In liberal sociology, human free will is not a critical concept and can, under certain circumstances, even be problematic. This is especially true when individuals try to act in ways which do not promote the collective. It is up to individuals to subordinate themselves to the corporate social structure to increase the likelihood of survival.

Since liberals do not believe in the existence of God, they hold that there is no such thing as an objective moral law which can guide a culture. It is entirely up to the society itself to decide what moral values will best contribute to survival. In actual practice, it becomes society's leaders who primarily lead in making the decisions on this front.

Primary Societal Institutions

In liberal sociology, the most important institution is the state. Since naturalistic belief prioritizes the collective above the individual, the institution which has the best means for ordering society in a way which promotes survival is the government. All other social institutions, then, are subservient to the state and should be organized and used based on the best judgment of those who are society's leaders.

It is also possible that, over time, the particular circumstances of society might change. If that happens, the importance or character of various societal institutions may also need to change to fit the new situation. In this case, there is no compelling reason societal values and rules can't be modified to meet the new situation.

How Liberal Sociology is Expressed in the Culture
Government

Government, in liberal sociology, is generally considered the most important of society's institutions. That is because it is the one which is best placed to guide the species to achieve survival over the long term.

As the survival of society is the highest value in liberalism, the needs of the collective stand above the desires and needs of the individual. As such, liberals generally believe that government should be structured in a way which allows it to have ultimate control over individuals.

While liberals believe there is no particular "right" way to structure government, the most prominent modern systems which fit naturalistic presuppositions are communism, socialism and progressivism. These governmental forms assure that the government has the power it needs to control society while helping to ensure equal outcomes for the members of society.

Family

In liberal sociology, with no belief in any kind of supernatural reality, all notions about humanity and human nature must be based on the belief that human beings are natural animals which exist in a purely naturalistic environment. As such, the only purpose of sexual relations is personal pleasure and to insure the survival of the species.

Liberals generally understand the family unit to be the most functional institution for raising the young. However, there is no particular reason why the family has to be structured as a traditional nuclear family. They do not believe in any kind of objective morality which would dictate a particular form of family structure. If plural marriage, homosexual marriage, common law marriage, or even no marriage "works" in a given situation, there is no reason these can't be accepted as legitimate family structures within the society. The only constraint would be a situation which somehow threatens the survival of the species.

Church

Liberal sociology begins with belief that there is no such thing as God. As such, liberals believe that no faith institution has any value other than to promote cohesion within the society. They see church to be nothing more than a means of social interaction, no different from any other social club that humans choose to create.

Education

Naturalistic beliefs govern education in liberal sociology, so there is no such thing as objective "truth" in a moral sense. Liberals believe that the material universe and natural processes are all that exist, so they must gear all education toward promoting knowledge which fits within that paradigm. Education must be focused on advancing ideas and beliefs which ensure the survival of society based on the current assessment of its leaders.

More specifically, historical material may be emphasized or de-emphasized as it helps governmental leaders disperse knowledge and information to promote their agenda. Additionally, liberals see science and technology to be important, but it may only be pursued based on naturalistic presuppositions. Liberals also believe it is permissible for the government to determine which subjects are needed to promote societal goals and to discourage the ones not aligned with its plans.

News Media

Based on liberal sociology, the work of the news media is to support the needs of society based on the understanding of those who lead. Since naturalistic thought does not recognize "objective truth," broadcasting truth is not the goal of the news media, unless those in leadership feel that helps promote society's survival. Overall, the primary goal of the news media is to share news and information which advances the vision and purposes of society's leaders in ways which promote survival.

Entertainment

Entertainment, based on liberal sociological thought, is purely for enjoyment. Liberals do not believe in any kind of objective morality, so nothing is automatically out of bounds based on moral constraints. There may be things which society deems inappropriate for certain groups, but it bases this evaluation on what its leaders believe will promote the survival of society at the time.

Medicine

Liberal sociology believes man is nothing more than a material animal subject to natural law. As liberals believe human survival is the highest value, the medical industry is important as an instrument to promote that goal. Liberals primarily see this as a collective societal issue, not an individual one. Thus, the importance of the medical industry is not to help individuals, but to make sure the species survives. Individual care is only valuable as it promotes the collective purpose.

Agriculture

Liberal sociology looks at agriculture in terms of the survival of the society. As such, it is the government's responsibility to determine what crops are grown, as well as prices and the means of distribution. The goal is to make sure that products are distributed throughout society in a way which ensures survival. Some liberals believe it is immoral for individual farmers to get rich farming because food is an essential survival commodity which belongs to the collective.

Law Enforcement

One important function of government, based on liberal beliefs, is to promote order. A key institution for handling this duty is law enforcement. The purpose of law enforcement, then, is not to provide for individual protection and justice. Rather, it is to make sure that the collective is in the best position for survival. It is up to government leaders, then, to use law enforcement in ways which promote the common good as they define it.

Businesses/Corporations

Since liberal sociology is based on the priority of the collective, the primary purpose of business is to make sure that the goods and services needed for the survival of society are produced and properly distributed. Liberals believe that management of production and distribution, however, should not be in the hands of private individuals. Rather, those responsible for overseeing the welfare of the collective (those in government) should be in charge. Liberals believe government should provide guidance and capital for the businesses which help accomplish its overall goals.

Chapter 10
Psychology

"Hello, Sally. I wasn't sure you were going to make it today," Lance declared as Sally hurried in, obviously out of breath. "You, okay?"

"Yeah, I'm fine," Sally responded. "Just running a bit late. I sort of ran over here. Didn't realize how out of shape I was."

Sally plopped down in the diner booth and began to open the menu.

"I took the liberty of going ahead and ordering your usual tea," Lance offered. "Hope that is what you wanted."

"Perfect," Sally replied. And as if on cue, the waitress brought their drinks. As they already knew what they wanted, she also went ahead and took their orders.

"Sally, tell me something," Lance began. He wasn't necessarily looking to begin a conversation on this topic, but had a concern about one of their colleagues and wanted more information. "I heard that Bill Freeman over in the math department had a nervous breakdown. Do you know anything about that? I know you guys are good friends."

"Yeah, I just went and saw him yesterday. He's been dealing with a lot of stress lately – trouble with his wife, financial issues, and one of his kids is even having drug problems. I guess all of that would cause just about anybody to break."

"Hmm, I had no idea he was dealing with all of that. So, what are they doing to treat him?"

"Actually, at this point, there is a bit of conflict about how to treat him" Sally explained. "John, over in the psychology department, is advising his wife to let Dr. Carlson, over at Psyc Inc., treat him. But her pastor is advising her to use the Christian counselor at their church. Bill never has gone to church with her and she is not sure quite what to do. I hope she goes with John's advice. I would hate for him to get hooked up with some religious charlatan."

"I know Dr. Williams over at Bill's wife's church," Lance countered. "He has his Ph.D. in psychology and is well respected. Why would you dis him like that?"

"Listen, Lance," Sally looked up at him with a bit of concern, "Bill and I grew up together. I have known him for a long time and am really worried about him. I just don't trust those religious people when it comes to professional care."

"So, Sally," Lance answered back, "what do you think will be different or inferior about the work of one psychologist over the other?"

Sally knew she and Lance had bumped up against another one of those issues where they were going to disagree because of their worldview beliefs. Still, she didn't see any reason to tippy-toe around the issue. "Okay, Lance," Sally began, "I know that if the religious psychologist works with him, he is going to suggest that God can help him. Now, I suppose that helping people reconcile their problems based on a fantasy is not an evil thing, but it is certainly not necessary. Why not do the work based on the truth?"

Lance listened to Sally give her explanation and replied back. "So, you would rather he be treated by someone who will work with him based on purely naturalistic presuppositions. Don't offer him hope and the possibility of peace with God, but to just reconcile his issues based on the 'reality' that this cold hard world is all there is. Is that what you are saying?"

"That's exactly what I am saying," Sally answered.

"So, Sally," Lance continued, "how do you know that using the naturalistic approach is the best way? Beyond that, how do you know that it is actually the truth? I believe just the opposite. I think that not recognizing the objectively true reality that God exists is one of the things that drives people to this state in the first place. It is being connected with God that can help them get healed."

"Lance," Sally shot back, "it is one thing to play your conservative religious games when it comes to political debates, but we are talking about a person's life here. You can't really be serious about them using that quack, can you?"

"I'm sorry, Sally, but this is one place where you are totally misguided," Lance offered back. "God is an objective reality. It is your naturalistic worldview beliefs which are the fantasy. If you want

Bill to truly get well, you better hope they use someone who is in touch with actual reality."

After that start, neither Sally nor Lance felt much like getting into a deep discussion. They mostly chit-chatted while they ate. Shortly after they finished, they decided to go ahead and leave. Neither was upset at the other, but this had been a rather disturbing conversation in many ways. They agreed that they would meet again the next week, but both of them carried away a bit of tension as they left.

****

The word "psychology" literally means the study of the soul. This is a rather interesting fact since modern secular approaches to psychology do not even recognize that a soul exists. That being said, there are elements of the human person that, while we cannot access them directly using empirical methods, are expressions of human life which cannot be ignored. Psychology deals most specifically with the mind, mental states and mental processes, and tries to discern how these interact with human behavior. Conservative and liberal notions about psychology are very different because they have radically different beliefs about the nature of the human person.

Conservative Psychology

For conservatives, an understanding of psychology is based on the principles of Christian Theism. It relates to both an objectively real spiritual element as well as a physical one. Conservatives believe that humans are spiritual as well as physical beings. Thus, they believe that a dualistic understanding of mind and body best explains the makeup of humanity. Conservative psychology operates from the belief that God made humans to be self-conscious spiritual beings housed in a physical body.

The soul is that part of a human being which is specifically not physical. So, when an individual has a matter which troubles the soul, it is a spiritual problem, not a physical one. More specifically, it relates to a person's sin against God, not to generic mental or emotional issues which cause internal conflict. Thus, the solution to problems regarding the soul requires making things right with him.

At the same time, the soul exists in a physical body and cannot be separated from it. We must understand and express the soul through the physical body. As such, there is a physiological element that comes into play, as well.

The conservative understanding of psychology places responsibility for personal morality on the shoulders of the individual, works to right a broken relationship with God, and gives meaning to human suffering. Rather than trying to mask emotional pain or transfer guilt to someone or something else, conservatives believe psychology should work toward solving the real problem – the spiritual issue which causes separation from God.

Human Nature

As with all of the other areas of life, a conservative understanding of human nature emerges out of a biblical worldview foundation. Based on this set of beliefs, conservatives understand human beings to be physical as well as spiritual beings. Thus, what happens in the body can affect the soul and vice versa. People must grapple with both parts if they wish to deal effectively with human psychology.

As human beings live life, dramatic physiological changes do occur over time in their brains. In spite of that, people typically retain their identity, memory, and ability to operate as free moral agents. This is an indication that the mind and the brain are not the same.

Still, conservatives do recognize a possible physiological element in the study and practice of psychology. The physical part relates to instances where a person's brain is somehow damaged. Certain kinds of impairment due to trauma or chemical imbalance can affect a person's memory and sense of personal identity. In these cases, part of the remedy may involve the use of medical technology.

That being said, the basic issue, when it comes to dealing with psychological problems, relates to spiritual, not physical, matters. Conservatives believe there is something within the human person that is fundamentally flawed which causes people to act contrary to what they know is right.

The cause of that internal flaw is sin. Sin, in this case, is not defined by mere moral or legal regulations. Rather, it is an objectively real spiritual principle which infects human nature at the level of the soul. Sin cannot be observed directly using scientific tools. Instead, it is observed indirectly in the lives of people as they struggle with life's moral issues. This affects individuals by creating conflict within their minds.

Psychological issues are essentially problems of the heart, not merely wrong thinking and behavior. And, since human beings are morally responsible before God, the essential fix is spiritual, not physical.

Guilt

Based on conservative psychology, God is a real person and rebellion against him is an actual offense which results in objective guilt. When people rebel against God they are guilty. The *feelings* of guilt they experience are simply the natural outworking of that objective guilt in an individual's consciousness. It is the spiritual equivalent of the physical pain people feel when their bodies are injured.

The foundational conservative belief about this topic, based on the teachings of the Bible, is that God provided the actual means of forgiveness for sin by the sacrificial death of Jesus Christ on the cross. When individuals ask God's forgiveness based on the death and resurrection of Christ, God actually declares them "not guilty." Then, as they develop a lifestyle which puts sin aside, the sources of psychological problems become less and less.

Conservative psychology does not simply try to explain away feelings of guilt. It points to the means for actually correcting the problem which brought it on in the first place. For conservatives, confession of sin and repentance toward God are the real cure for human psychological problems.

Mental Illness is Physiological

The fact that psychological problems are essentially spiritual does not eliminate the notion of mental illness. There are problems which are caused by brain damage, tumors, chemical disorders and the like. These, though, fall into a different category than the problems caused by acts of rebellion against God. People who have no physiological problems are not really mentally ill. They are merely people with some kind of unresolved sin issue.

The Problem of Suffering

In the minds of many, any kind of suffering, physical or mental, is the enemy. Using this assumption, the way to overcome problems is to do whatever it takes to end the suffering. Based on conservative beliefs, however, suffering is not a problem in and of itself. In fact, it serves two important functions.

First, suffering may be a symptom of some kind of spiritual (psychological) illness. If a person experiences this type of suffering, simply concluding that the sin is not real, as in liberal psychology, merely masks symptoms. It is like taking aspirin to keep a cut from hurting. It may mask the pain, but will not cure the cut. If suffering is because of sin, the only cure is to receive forgiveness.

But in conservative psychology there is also another kind of suffering. Conservatives recognize that God sometimes uses suffering to bring about growth or positive change. Sometimes God permits suffering in people's lives to strengthen them or to help them develop discipline. In God's economy, everything must be redeemed in order for the sin problem to be overcome. This includes suffering. Conservative psychology believes every kind of suffering, no matter how horrific, can be used to accomplish a greater good.

How Conservative Psychology is Expressed in the Culture
Dealing with Individual Psychological Problems

In conservative thinking, actions which go against biblical morality are considered bad and are the source of conflict within the minds of individuals. Thus, for conservatives, things such as murder, arson, sex outside marriage, homosexual behavior, covetousness, gluttony, and any other kind of anti-biblical behavior create feelings of guilt which are the source of psychological issues. This puts individual responsibility for solving psychological problems front and center.

This does not mean, however, that trained counselors are useless. In fact, the help of counselors can be very beneficial for many people. That being said, true help involves the counselor leading people to recognize how sin is creating disorder. Treatment, on a personal level, needs to be dealt with as a spiritual issue. With that, a counselor can help people grasp how to align their lives with God's purposes.

Societal handling of psychological problems

According to conservative beliefs, psychological issues can create problems within the larger culture as the wrong actions of individuals spill over to affect other people. Psychological issues which bring people to a state so that they are no longer able to function within society may create the need for government or private organizations to establish institutions, programs, or laws to deal with them.

Liberal Psychology

Psychology in liberalism is based on the naturalistic belief that human beings are purely physical animals with no spiritual part. Thus, the soul, in liberal psychology, is nothing more than the physical self. This understanding leads to methods of dealing with the human mind and human behavior which are purely physiological. Using the common naturalistic approaches to psychology, curing human psychological problems is a matter of fixing wrong thinking by using behavioral techniques and medicines.

Since Naturalism does not acknowledge the existence of a supernatural reality, all of the elements that people associate with the idea of soul are necessarily physical in nature. That is, the human sense of self-consciousness and free will are nothing more than the functioning of a physical brain which has evolved to a level complex enough to give that illusion. As a result, liberal psychology involves learning techniques for manipulating the brain which can do away with the emotional pain that human beings experience in life.

One critical issue in liberal psychology involves discerning what makes up normal and abnormal psychological behavior. Since liberals don't recognize any kind of objective morality, they believe people must evaluate what is normal and abnormal based on what contributes to or breaks down a given societal grouping. Proper behavior, as is the case with proper morality, is relative to the situation and can change over time as circumstances change. The evaluation of right and wrong must be based on the contemporary beliefs of the majority in society or the preferences of those who hold political power.

Human Nature

Based on their naturalistic worldview beliefs, those who practice liberal psychology do not believe there is any kind of objective spiritual element to the human animal. Thus, human nature is purely animal nature. Since liberals believe that the human brain naturally evolved to become complex enough to provide a sense of free will and self-consciousness, human beings are able to consider possibilities of behavior which are not possible for creatures with less complex brains.

Since humans are, in their most basic essence, purely physical animals with no spiritual part, all behaviors associated with the animal nature are morally neutral. There is no such thing as any kind of objective moral stigma to any behavior. That being said, individuals and societies do develop their own codes of morality which can be violated by individuals. These violations can create inner conflict which need to somehow be resolved.

Guilt

In liberal psychology, there is no such thing as guilt in an objective sense. Objective guilt requires an objective morality which liberals don't accept. For them, guilt is simply a feeling that something is not right.

Thus, the sense of guilt that some people experience can be nothing more than wrong thinking. The remedy, then, is simply to learn how to think differently to end the mental pain.

Thus, for liberal psychologists, the primary approach for solving guilt problems is either to help people come to a realization that the action(s) which brought on the guilt feelings is not actually bad, or help them change behavior in a way that allows them to avoid the feelings.

In liberal psychology, there is no objectively "right or wrong" way to help people with their problems. Liberals generally believe, though, that the best means to accomplish healing are those which bring conformity to the currently accepted laws and mores of society.

The Problem of Suffering

In liberal psychology, mental suffering is, itself, the enemy. It is that sense of suffering which must be eliminated at all costs. Since liberals believe there is no objective meaning associated with human life, there can be no objective purpose for suffering. Whatever it takes to overcome the feelings of suffering is considered legitimate and is the road to a cure.

How Liberal Psychology is Expressed in the Culture
Dealing with Individual Psychological Problems
In liberal thought, since society holds priority over the individual, what is morally appropriate is whatever society holds to be acceptable. As such, the source of psychological conflict arises out of issues which have their root in societal morality rather than offense to God.

In liberal psychology, mental suffering is considered the enemy. Liberals identify psychological issues by observing what causes mental pain within individuals. Success in dealing with these issues occurs when the distress is eliminated.

The work of trained counselors, then, is the work of socialization. Liberals believe that individuals are helped as they learn to accept and live in harmony with society's rules. By reconciling people's thoughts to the standards of society, they are able to eliminate internal conflict. Since liberals believe all remedies must be physiological, they believe they can generate psychological cures using only medication or behavioral techniques.

Societal Handling of Psychological Problems
As is true with conservatives, liberals also believe that the psychological issues of individuals can create problems within the larger culture as antisocial actions spill over to affect others. When that happens, society may have to take damage control measures by setting up institutions or creating laws to deal with them. In the case of liberal psychology, since the collective takes precedence over the individual, it is much easier to curtail antisocial behavior by putting people into institutions or by medicating them.

Chapter 11
Communication

"Lance, did you hear the president's speech last night? That had to be one of the best speeches I have ever heard," Sally gushed as she downed a French fry. As was their practice these days, Sally and Lance were having their usual Thursday discussion at the diner.

"Sally," Lance countered, "I know you are enthralled that we now have a liberal president, and I will grant you that he is talented at giving speeches, but how can you bear to even listen to him. Hardly a word of truth ever passes his lips."

"Oh come on Lance," Sally jabbed, "you are not still being a sore loser, are you?"

"You know, I certainly don't like losing, but there is something here that goes well beyond simply not wanting to lose," Lance replied rather pensively. "I believe that this guy is actually harming the country. And one of the reasons he is getting away with so much is because of the manner in which he uses communication."

"What do you mean by that, Lance?" Sally queried, a bit intrigued by this turn of the conversation. "Are you just jealous that he is able to use social media so well and that he has such good access to the radio and TV markets?"

"Nah, none of that," Lance responded. "Obviously, he does have that stuff down pretty doggone well, and those are important elements of the communication process. But my concern goes much deeper than that. I don't think he tells the truth. He parses words in ways which make it seem like he is saying one thing when he really means something else. On top of that, he uses vocabulary which means one thing to the people who are hearing it, but has an entirely different meaning to him – just to make people think they agree with him when they really don't. And finally, he implements policies which are simply wrong or illegal, then purely lies as he tries to justify himself to the public. Honestly, he uses very sophisticated propaganda techniques in his communication to lead people down a very bad path."

With such straight talk, Sally was kind of taken back. She didn't very often see that kind of passion coming from Lance. That was usually more her thing. "Lance, you are making way more of this than you ought to. It is not that big a deal. The president has some very, very important goals that he is trying to get accomplished. And, as you know, he has a lot of resistance from your conservative comrades. He has to do things to try to work around all the haters. If he can use communication techniques which counteract his detractors, what's the big deal?"

"What's the big deal," Lance whipped back, "is that he is not telling the truth. He is manipulating people."

Sally tried to reason with him. "Lance, people do that all the time. In this case his ideas and policies are so important that they need to be implemented. If he turns a phrase in a way which makes his point of view sound more reasonable to more people, there is no harm in that."

"No Sally," Lance rebutted, "there is harm in it. There is such a thing as truth and people need to be straightforward with it. It is certainly possible to use persuasive speech without being deceptive. I have a real problem with his approach."

"Well, Lance," Sally countered, "we will just have to agree to disagree on this point. If it helps him accomplish his important agenda, I don't see anything wrong with using creative wordsmithing."

"Well, I guess we will have to disagree on this one," Lance replied. "A lie is a lie, I don't care how creatively it is spoken."

"Oh, before I forget," Lance quickly changed the subject, "you had mentioned that you wanted to attend one of the Conservative Council meetings so you could meet all of the hayseeds. We have one coming up in a couple of weeks, want to go? We will be discussing the Theory of Evolution."

"Hmm, that sounds like an interesting one. Sure, put me down," Sally responded. "I don't have to be on a panel, do I?"

Lance smiled and replied, "No, I won't do that to you."

"Oh my," Sally saw the clock on the wall and noticed she was running late. "I have an appointment in five minutes in my office. Sorry I have to run so quickly today. See you next week?"

"Great! Sounds good," Lance replied. "I'll get your ticket so you can get going. You can get mine another time."

"Thanks, Lance. You are a great friend – even if you do have convoluted ideas." At that they both chuckled as Sally hurried away.

****

Communication deals with the way human beings convey meaning to one another. People communicate with others in a broad variety of ways – everything from face-to-face conversations to the use of mass media. Communication deals both with the mechanics of conveying meaning, and with the actual ideas people want to share. Individuals express meaning to others based on their religious, political, cultural, economic, and social identities.

Conservative Communication

Conservative communication begins with the belief that human beings are creatures made in the image of God. This includes the fact that humans are persons who are self-conscious and have a legitimate free will. Having these capabilities allows human beings to compose thoughts independently and express those thoughts to others who have that same capability. Those able to participate in the communication process include not only human persons, but also God himself.

Conservatives also recognize a moral element to the communication process. As God has revealed an objectively true morality to mankind, communication should be used in a way that corresponds with God's desires.

Self-Talk

In conservative belief, God created human beings as self-aware persons. That means they are able to recognize self as an individual separate from the environment and from other individuals. The result of that kind of self-awareness is that humans have the ability to spontaneously compose ideas and personally consider the implications of those ideas.

Interpersonal Communication

Conservatives recognize that self-awareness not only has personal implications, but that it provides the platform for interpersonal communication, as well. Since all persons, other than those with special disabilities, have the capacity to communicate, individuals can share thoughts and ideas with other persons.

The ability to self-consciously communicate with others opens up a wide variety of communication possibilities. It is possible to communicate personal matters, as well as other information, in order to inform, persuade or motivate people.

Mass Communication

Communication may also take place using impersonal platforms. This can involve anything from the use of broadcast media, such as TV and radio, to the internet, newspapers, magazines, and film. Conservatives see the use of mass media as a means by which self-aware persons may convey information to other self-aware persons. They generally understand the means of communication to be morally neutral. At the same time, they do judge the content of messages based on how it aligns with the moral teachings of the Bible.

Prayer

Conservatives believe that communication can be expressed between any self-aware persons who are able to communicate. This includes not only human beings, but supernatural spiritual beings, as well. As such, humans, because they are spiritual persons created in the image of God, are capable of communicating with him using language by prayer.

How Conservative Communication is Expressed in Culture
Communication with Other Human Beings

Conservatives understand human beings to be self-aware, free-will persons who are able to share and receive meaningful communications between themselves. Communication can take many forms including: personal contemplation within one's own mind, the sharing of personal thoughts face-to-face with others, directly providing information to a group, attempts to persuade others, or even the use of mass communication technologies to inform and persuade.

But for conservatives, the issues related to communication are not just about the means for communicating. They also involve the content of the messages. As conservatives consider human beings to be specially created by God to fulfill a purpose, the communication they express ought to be purposeful and in line with God's will. This means that communication ought to reflect what is true and right based on standards expressed in the Bible.

Communication with God

Conservative beliefs about communication begin with the idea that God created man in his own image with the ability to communicate with other persons. Built into that belief is the notion that man can also communicate with God. In fact, the biblical revelation expresses that one of God's primary reasons for creating man was that they might enjoy one another's fellowship. As such, conservatives believe communicating with God is an important element of human life.

Liberal Communication

Liberal communication begins with the belief that human beings are purely material animals which have naturally evolved to their current state. As such, the capacity for self-consciousness and free will are completely the result of naturalistic evolution. Liberals believe the human brain has evolved to a level where this kind of information processing is possible. Liberals debate among themselves whether this capability is actual or is merely an illusion based on evolutionary brain development. In any case, having these capabilities allow human beings to have thoughts which they are able to communicate to other persons who have that same capability.

Self-Talk

Liberals begin with the belief that human beings are naturally evolved animal creatures. As such, it was purely an accident of nature that humans became the kind of creature that now exists. There is no reason or purpose behind it.

It just so happens that in the evolutionary development of the human species, the capacity for self-awareness emerged. Whether this is actual self-awareness or is an illusion based on the complexity of the human brain is of no consequence. At the very least, humans seem self-aware. As such, they may use that capacity to consider their personal lives in the world.

Interpersonal Communication

Liberals believe that human beings have evolved the capacity for self-awareness and that it provides a platform for interpersonal communication. Humans can use this ability to convey meaningful ideas to other humans on a wide range of platforms – from a very personal level to impersonal broadcasts. People can use this communication process to inform, persuade or motivate.

Mass Communication

The actual use of the mechanics of mass communication technologies is no different for liberals than for conservatives. As such, it can involve anything from the use of broadcast media, such as TV and radio, to the internet, newspapers, magazines, and film.

What liberals may evaluate differently is the content of communications. As they do not acknowledge any such thing as objectively real morality, the concept of communication as inherently moral or immoral is meaningless. The morality of the communication can only be judged by how it affects the survival of the society.

How Liberal Communication is Expressed in Culture
Communication with Other Human Beings

As liberals believe there is no such thing as a supernatural reality, the very notion of interacting with God is absurd on its face. They understand human beings to be naturally evolved animal creatures. As such, they understand the communication process to be purely an evolutionary development which enhances the survivability of the human race. Based on the current state of evolutionary development in the world, liberals recognize that self-conscious communication only takes place between human beings. This could change over time as other creatures evolve more complex brains.

Since there is no such thing as an objectively true morality, liberals do not see any kind of absolute moral component to the act of communication. It is simply a mechanical process humans use in whatever way they deem appropriate. The appropriateness of any

communication is based on the personal preferences of individuals
or by those who control the means of communication in society, not
on any kind of absolute concept of truth.

Chapter 12
Ethics and Morality

Lance was just getting ready to leave his office and head home when the phone rang. "Hello, this is Lance, how can I help you?" Lance immediately recognized the voice on the other end. "Hey, this is Sally. I would like to talk with you about something. Would you be able to drop by my house for a few minutes before you head home?"

Lance thought a second and said, "Yeah, I guess so. You just caught me as I was getting ready to walk out the door. Is everything okay?"

"Yeah, I'm fine. I just need to talk with you a few minutes," Sally answered back.

"Okay. You are pretty close," Lance replied. "I should be able to get over to your house in about ten minutes or so. See you in a few."

As Lance locked the office and headed to his car, he wondered what in the world was going on with Sally. "Well, I guess I will find out in a few minutes," he thought.

About ten minutes later Lance pulled up to the front of Sally's house, got out of his car, walked up on her porch and knocked. Straight away, Sally opened the door and invited him in. "Come on in and have a seat in the living room," she offered.

As they walked into the living room, Lance was impressed with the nice layout of Sally's house. He walked across the room and sat down on a nice comfortable easy chair. Sally took her seat across from him on the couch.

"What's up," Lance asked with a look of concern on his face. "I hope everything is okay."

"Oh yeah, I'm fine," Sally responded. "I just have something I wanted to ask you. I hope you won't be offended by this. I have really enjoyed getting to know you better in our discussions, even though we don't seem to agree on much. You are very well spoken, and if you don't mind me saying so, are a nice looking guy, as well." When she said that, Sally paused to watch his expression. Lance was caught off guard with this turn of the conversation and blushed a little. She continued, "Have you been enjoying it, too?"

Lance began to feel a little uncomfortable, but he answered, "Well, yes. I have enjoyed it very much. What are you getting at?"

"Well, Lance, you know my history," Sally picked up where she had left off. "I was married several years ago and it didn't work out well. When I divorced, I decided that I didn't want to get married again. I guess you can say I am married to my work. Still, I do enjoy certain 'benefits' of marriage, if you get what I mean. I just wanted to ask you if you would like to have a romantic relationship with me. Like I said, I don't want to be married and I don't want to interfere with your relationship with your family. We could do it without any strings. Consider it 'friends with benefits.'"

At this, Lance was caught completely off guard. This was totally unexpected. But he collected himself and responded tactfully, "Sally, I am very flattered by your offer. I really do enjoy your company and you are certainly a very beautiful woman. But I am going to have to decline your offer. This simply does not correspond with how I view my relationship with my wife, and my relationship with God."

"I thought you might respond that way," Sally confessed as she continued her appeal. "I am really serious about there not being any strings."

"I know you mean it Sally," Lance replied, "but I don't think you fully understand where I am coming from. Even this goes back to our worldview foundations. Since you begin with naturalistic presuppositions, you see human relationships only in terms of the physical and emotional intercourse of physical beings. But I really do believe that God is an objectively real person. I love him and want to please him. A relationship with another woman outside of my marriage does not correspond with how I understand appropriate relationships. I simply can't do that to my wife or to God.

"Lance Jackson, you really are a puzzle to me," Sally responded. "Listen, I know I have created a very uncomfortable situation for you and am truly sorry. Will you please forgive my indiscretion? We really do see relationships differently. I honestly don't see anything wrong with it, but I do respect your personal convictions. The thing I am most concerned about, now, is that I hope this will not keep us from continuing our talks. I promise I won't ever flirt with you in a tempting way, and will never bring this up again. I will just go and find another partner to meet my needs. Can you please forgive me and forget this ever happened?"

"I understand, Sally," Lance replied. "I will take you at your word and will forget this ever happened. I do enjoy our conversations and look forward to getting back on track next week."

At that, Lance headed outside and walked to his car. "Wow," he thought, "that really took my breath away."

****

Ethics is the study of morality and is a system of moral principles and rules of conduct which are recognized and followed by a group of people. It deals with the values which underlie human conduct regarding what is right and wrong, good and bad. The moral principles which determine what is ethical and what is not is squarely based upon a person's, or group's, worldview assumptions.

Conservative Ethics and Morality

Conservative ethics, established on a Theistic worldview foundation, are based on a belief in moral absolutes. Theism believes in a supernatural God who has revealed to mankind what is right and wrong. Conservatives believe God has a particular way he wants people to act, and has revealed that desire to humanity. In the case of American conservatism, that relates specifically to the values revealed in the Bible.

The notion of sin also plays an important part in conservative ethics. As was explained before, based on Christian Theism, conservatives believe human beings are fallen creatures who have been overtaken by sin. They see lapses in ethics, then, to be the result of the sin problem playing out in the lives of human beings. There are three important implications which flow from a conservative view of ethics.

First, conservatives recognize that there is a good and right way to live which is based on the very character of God and revealed in the Bible. As such, ethics have an absolute, unchangeable foundation. When humans fail, conservative ethics require acknowledgment of the failure and holds that it should be made right, whatever that takes. When an ethical failure affects another person, that needs to be made right, as well.

Second, individuals must choose to live out what is good and right. The actions people take in life are based on free-will decisions. When individuals decide to live according to the teachings in God's revelation, they put themselves in a position to live in fellowship with him.

Finally, conservatives believe that human beings must have an attitude of gratitude toward God. That only comes by living in relationship with him. Simply knowing what is right does not give individuals the power to live rightly. People who recognize their dependence upon God, and willfully live life in that dependence, cannot help but be grateful that he makes it possible for them to follow the ethical principles he has revealed.

How Conservative Ethics is Expressed in the Culture
Honesty and Integrity
As conservative morality is based on the character of God, his revelation becomes the place people must look to determine how to act. The Bible portrays God as a person of truth and integrity who implores human beings to live likewise. Conservatives expect this to be reflected in the personal life of every individual and in every societal institution.

Sexual Morality
Conservative sexual ethics are based on the morality revealed in the Bible. Conservatives believe any sexual relationship other than one that occurs within the bonds of marriage between one man and one woman is wrong.

Social Relationships
Based on conservative ethics, human relationships, at every level, are important because human beings are considered God's highest creation and hold highest value. As such, conservatives believe relationships should be based on respect and characterized by honesty and integrity.

Use of Language

Conservatives believe God created mankind in his own image. This involves the ability to communicate using language. Essentially, language is nothing more than a tool which individuals use to convey meaning to others. As such, it can be used rightly or wrongly. People can use it to convey thoughts and ideas which reflect God's purposes, but also those which run counter to God. A conservative approach expects that people will use language in ways which reflect God's character and purposes.

Human Life

Conservative ethics value what God values as reflected in the teachings of the Bible. Since God created mankind in his own image, human life is of highest value to him. As such, conservatives believe actions which destroy human life, such as abortion, euthanasia, and murder, are wrong. Similarly, conservatives consider tampering with human life by human cloning and embryonic stem cell research to be meddling with life in a way which is not the prerogative of human beings. Capital punishment does not fall into the category of individual ethics as that is a function of the state.

Economics

Based on biblical teachings, there is a way that people should think of and use material resources. The most basic conservative belief regarding economics is that everything ultimately belongs to God. Human beings are to act as his stewards by using material resources based on his purposes. Since free market economics puts resources primarily under the control of private individuals, conservatives generally believe it is the best approach for dealing with economics. That being said, it is the responsibility of individuals to discern God's will and use the resources based on biblical moral principles.

Aesthetics and Entertainment

It is possible to express both biblical and non-biblical morality through aesthetics and entertainment. Conservatives view morality through the lens of biblical teachings and believe individuals should only support or participate in entertainment which promotes biblical morality.

Intellect

It is possible for individuals to express their intellectual capacity based on different codes of morality. Conservative morality promotes a use of the intellect which strives for truth and excellence as expressed in the biblical revelation.

Religion

In general, morality is based on an individual's religious beliefs. As conservative morality is based on Christian Theism, it is focused specifically on the moral precepts of the Christian faith as revealed in the Bible.

Liberal Ethics and Morality

Liberal ethics emerges out of Naturalism and is based on the concept of moral relativism. Liberals acknowledge no form of supernatural existence. As such, there is no one outside the material universe able to create or share moral information. That being the case, human beings must create all morality and ethics. They may do this either by using personal preference, societal consensus or the strong arm of those in power. Since liberals do not believe in moral absolutes, the standards of morality may change as the societal situation or the individuals in power change.

Essentially, liberal ethics assert that morality is strictly a man-made set of behavioral rules and are relative to the situation. As human beings are the only creatures able to self-consciously consider ethics, they must make up their own morality. As a result, ethics become nothing more than what is functional for society or is satisfying for self.

How Liberal Ethics is Expressed in the Culture
Honesty and Integrity

Since liberal morality has no absolute foundation, human beings must determine for themselves what rules work most effectively to keep society ordered. Morality is purely based on functionality, not on any kind of objective right and wrong. The very concept of honesty and integrity have no objective foundation, so there is nothing innately immoral about being dishonest. The primary focus is not what is right, but what works. If honesty and integrity work in a particular situation, that may become the standard. If it does not work to achieve one's personal, or society's, goals, dishonesty and lack of integrity may be acceptable.

Sexual Morality

Liberal sexual ethics are based on naturalistic presuppositions. Based on this worldview foundation, there is no such thing as objective sexual immorality. For liberals, the determining factor for right and wrong regarding sexual relationships is how it affects the operation of society. In particular circumstances, any kind of sexual relations may be seen as acceptable – cohabitation, homosexual relationships, adultery, adult relationships with children, plural marriages, partner swapping, bestiality and any other expression. In other situations, society may believe some constraints are necessary to promote survival. Whatever is accepted will always be relative to the situation.

Social Relationships

In liberal morality, human relationships are based purely on functionality. If there is a reason for a relationship to exist, pursuing it can be considered good. Otherwise, there is no particular objective purpose for it. What is deemed good is that which is seen to be best for the survival of society.

Use of Language

Liberal ethics associates no particular moral element to language. Liberals approach the use of language in whatever way seems to further their personal, or society's, agenda. There isn't anything necessarily wrong with cursing or lying as long as it doesn't create negative effects in one's life or negatively affect the survival of the species.

Human Life

Liberal ethics views life as of ultimate value. That being said, it is not individual life that is valued, rather it is life generically as expressed in the collective. Liberals understand life to be a purely natural phenomenon without independent value. As such, the killing of a particular life may or may not be considered bad based on the circumstances.

Because of this kind of worldview foundation, there are particular lives which liberals can regard as expendable if society considers them as not having value. In the past, this kind of value system has led to the extermination of the elderly, the sick, certain races, certain social classes, certain families, people with certain political beliefs, the preborn, etc. This is the rationale for why abortion, euthanasia, human cloning, and rationing of medical care are not considered problematic in certain contexts. It is even possible that murder could be considered acceptable under the right circumstances.

Economics

Based on liberal moral teachings, all resources are ultimately the property of the collective to be used for the survival of society. As such, liberals believe collectivist economics, which puts resources primarily under the control of the government, is morally superior to an approach which favors the individual. That way, those in power can distribute resources in a way which they believe best benefits society.

Aesthetics and Entertainment

Liberal morality views aesthetics and entertainment through the lens of naturalistic beliefs. For liberals, there is no such thing as objective morality so literally anything goes in this arena. The only restraints would be those things that might be thought to bring harm to society.

Intellect

Liberal morality is not based on any kind of objective moral notion. As such, people are free to use their intellect to pursue anything they wish. The only restrictions would be those which are imposed by the ones who hold the reins of power.

Religion

Liberal ethics is based on Naturalism and does not recognize the existence of God. It follows, then, that there is no objective basis for morality. As such, liberals regard the very concept of religious morality as absurd. Religion may serve as a means of talking about morality, but there is nothing objectively real about it.

Chapter 13
Biology

The day for the next Conservative Council meeting had arrived. Sally was looking forward to seeing just how these folks were going to justify non-belief in the Theory of Evolution. Dr. Raymond Cahill, a noted Christian scholar, would be doing the presentation.

When Sally arrived at the lecture hall, Lance was already there waiting for her. The two exchanged greetings, then walked into the hall together. As Lance would be presiding over the meeting, he escorted Sally to the seats down front, then left her to go tend to his responsibilities. As she sat there, several colleagues from the university that she knew came to speak to her. She chatted with these friends until time for the meeting to start.

At that point, Lance called the meeting to order, delivered a few preliminaries, then called Dr. Cahill to the front to deliver his lecture. The main focus of his presentation was to share how Darwin's Theory of Evolution was not credible because it was not based on known science. He began with the premise that there is no experimental science to demonstrate that life could emerge from non-life – which would be necessary for naturalistic evolution to occur. Then, he went on to talk about how evolutionary biologists base their belief on naturalistic presuppositions, not on actual experimental science. He contended that Darwinian evolution was a philosophical position with no experimental science to back it up.

Close to the end of his lecture, he stopped and told the people in the audience to divide into small groups and take ten minutes to dialogue about what he had said. Lance came down to where Sally was sitting and suggested that they be a group themselves. "That would be great," Sally responded. She appreciated his consideration as she was already comfortable discussing things like that with him.

"So," Lance began, "what did you think?"

Sally wasted no time responding. "Hey, the whole talk was nothing but mumbo-jumbo. Who does he think he is saying there is no science to back up the theory? It is based on nothing but science."

"Sally," Lance answered, "you seem to have missed what he was saying. Let's start with the origin of life."

"Hold on, guy," Sally cut him off. "He made a cardinal mistake with that line. He is mixing up abiogenesis and the Theory of Evolution. They are not the same thing."

"Of course they are not," Lance responded. "But I think you missed the point. For Naturalists, without the emergence of life from non-life, there would be no life to evolve. And, since you Naturalists don't believe in a creator, abiogenesis is necessary. So that point is pertinent. How do you deal with that?"

Sally didn't even hesitate. "You already know the answer to that. Just because science doesn't yet know how it happened doesn't mean that the answers are not there. We just have to keep experimenting. It will come, you know."

"That is a wonderful statement of faith, Sally," Lance answered back. "That is as much a religious statement as my belief that God created life."

As they didn't have much more time, Lance thought it would be best to shift gears. "Sally," he continued, "before we run out of time, let's move on to the second part – that the Theory of Evolution itself is not based in experimental science."

"Lance," Sally shot back, "that is an even more ludicrous statement. There is a massive amount of scientific evidence to support naturalistic evolution – even to the point that we can practically say it has been proven."

"Wrong!" Lance retorted. "What you are referring to is the arrangement of facts. There certainly are artifacts which relate to this topic, but you can only say the evidence supports naturalistic evolution if your naturalistic presuppositions are true, and that is a BIG if. So, you are back to needing to prove your presuppositions – which is impossible because worldview beliefs cannot be proven empirically. There is no experimental science to prove naturalistic evolution is even possible. It is all based on belief."

Sally and Lance went back and forth for another five minutes until Dr. Cahill called attention back to himself. At that, he took another ten minutes to wrap up.

When he was finished, Lance went back to the podium, announced when the next meeting would be held and adjourned.

When he walked back down to speak to Sally, she was already heading over to talk to Dr. Cahill herself. By the time Lance got over to where the two of them were, they were already into a deep discussion. Lance briefly interrupted to thank Dr. Cahill and shake his hand. But, so as not to stop the discussion, he quickly excused himself and left them to talk. Lance knew he would hear more about that later.

****

The topic of biology relates to the study of life or living matter. More specifically, it deals with life's origin, growth, reproduction, structure, and behavior. It is, actually, rather difficult for people who hold different worldviews to understand how it is even possible to look at a topic like biology from a different perspective. That being said, there are different ways to deal with it based on different worldview foundations. In fact, the various understandings of the nature of ultimate reality require different ways of dealing with biology.

Conservative Biology
The conservative approach to understanding biology is based on Christian Theism. Using this worldview, the most fundamental belief about biology is that God created life. Conservatives see no problem believing that God created life AND that science can study the material expressions of life.

Biology is, of course, relevant to the study of both plant and animal life. As a point of particular interest, however, conservatives place a special emphasis on human life because of the belief that God created man in his own image.

When it comes to man, biology addresses only the physical elements of the human person. But conservatives also believe that God created human beings with a spiritual part which exists beyond biological exploration. As such, conservatives operate in two arenas. First, they take seriously the physical environment where biological science contributes to human understanding of physical life. Secondly, they believe human beings have a spiritual component which lies outside biological investigation.

Origins of Life

Conservative biology believes that God made an intentional decision to create physical life and built a material universe to house this life form. Life did not simply evolve out of non-life, but God, who is the source of life, inserted it into the physical creatures he created.

The Variety of Life

Conservative belief does not reject science as it relates to biology. It does, however, make a critical distinction between what biologists can empirically show and what they cannot. Micro-evolution (changes within living organisms which allow them to adapt to their environment – also called natural selection) can actually be shown based on experimental science. Contrary to the belief of most liberals, conservatives have no issue with any element of biological science which can be empirically demonstrated. Natural selection falls into this category.

But scientists have never shown that natural selection is a vehicle which can account for the variety of life on earth. The biological mechanisms within an organism which allows it to change in order to adapt to its environment is limited. There is a point beyond which it cannot continue. Conservative belief, based on a theistic foundation, understands life to be the special creation of God. As such, no life, and no life form, exists other than what God has created and sustains.

Value of Life

Based on biblical teachings, conservatives believe that since God created it, all of life has value. This includes all forms of plant and animal life.

But not all life is equally valuable. The conservative perspective is that God uniquely created human beings in his own image. As such, human life has special value. Based on biblical teachings, there are particular circumstances where the taking of human life is permissible. However, the taking of *innocent* human life is always considered morally wrong.

Conservatives also consider other forms of life to be valuable, but in a different way. When God created humans, he gave them dominion over the world that they should care for it. As such, human beings are to act as God's stewards over the entire created order, including other life forms. Humans may use other life for survival and as resources to improve human life, but may not deal with them in cruel or wasteful ways.

How Conservative Biology is Expressed in the Culture
Origins
The issue of origins shows up in culture primarily in school settings where the Theory of Evolution is taught in biology classes. Conservatives believe naturalistic evolution is as much a faith position as creationism and object to the fact that the teaching of naturalistic evolution in public schools is generally all that is allowed.

Based on a conservative point of view, the origin of life is found in the creative activity of God, not in naturalistic evolution. Conservatives also believe that human beings are a special creation of God. They do not understand why liberals so oppose the teaching of creationism as a possible theory of origins since their own favorite theory is also based on faith.

Evolution/Variety of Life
The same is true when it comes to accounting for the variety of life forms on earth. Conservatives believe that the various life forms are direct creations of God. And, as with the topic of origins, conservatives don't understand why public schools cannot teach creation by God along with Darwinistic evolution since both are equally faith positions.

When it comes to actual experimental biology, there is virtually no difference in the beliefs of liberals and conservatives. Both believe in the objective reality of the material world and that it operates based on fixed natural laws.

Value of Life
In conservative belief, human life is of ultimate value because God made man as a special creation. As such, the taking of innocent human life is not acceptable. This principle applies in every arena – private and public. In the private arena, it is not acceptable for an individual to commit murder, abortion or euthanasia. Likewise, in the public arena, it is not acceptable for the state to take a human life unjustly. Capital punishment is permissible by the state to allow for

justice to be carried out appropriately. The distinctions for making these kinds of moral judgments are based on the teachings of the Bible.

For conservatives, other life is also valuable. As God's stewards, conservatives believe it is man's special responsibility to take care of the earth. This care includes other life forms. That being said, other life forms exist partially to sustain mankind. They can be legitimately used for food and as resources to improve the lives of humans.

Liberal Biology

Liberal biology is founded on Naturalism. Naturalism assumes that there is no such thing as a supernatural reality and that natural processes can account for all of material existence. This principle also applies to the existence and development of life. Liberals believe that life originated from inert chemicals and evolved to more complex forms based on naturalistic evolution.

Origins of Life

In liberal biology, everything must be explained naturally. Thus, life itself had to have originated by natural means. Although no one has ever been able to offer evidence of this theory by using experimental science, liberals recognize no other possibility. It must be that inert chemicals combined under the right circumstances to produce life.

The Variety of Life

Liberal biology also requires that the variety of life forms on earth had to have emerged through completely natural means. The term associated with this process is macro-evolution. This is the belief that natural selection occurs beyond what can actually be demonstrated based on experimental science. Liberals believe that less complex life forms can evolve to more complex forms over time. Even though there is no experimental science able to show this can actually occur, liberals assert it because they allow no other possibility.

Value of Life

Liberals do not believe in any supernatural reality, so no objective meaning or value can be associated with life. That is, there is no being to infuse meaning into it. Any meaning which is assigned to life must be done by humans themselves since they are the only creatures in existence able to make that kind of assessment.

Liberals base their judgment concerning the value of life on the belief that it is valuable simply because it exists. That is, the bottom line value is survival of the species. Based on this principle, individual life forms are less important than the species in general.

Additionally, since liberals believe all life forms have naturally evolved, they conclude that all are equally valuable. No special value can be assigned to any particular species. Because all life is equally valuable and human beings are the only creatures able to consciously understand that notion, liberals believe that humanity has a special responsibility to protect the survival of other life forms in the same way it looks to protect its own.

How Liberal Biology is Expressed in the Culture
Origins
Based on a liberal point of view, the only possibility for the origin of life is that it emerged naturally. Belief in a supernatural genesis is considered superstitious and unscientific. As such, teaching anything in educational institutions other than a naturalistic approach to origins is considered taboo.

Evolution/Variety of Life
The same is true when accounting for the variety of life forms on earth. Since liberals acknowledge no supernatural existence, they only accept a naturalistic approach to explaining the variety of life on earth. Since Darwinian evolution is the only theory available to make this case for Naturalism, liberals believe it should be the only approach schools are allowed to teach.

Value of Life
Since liberals believe no supernatural reality exists, there is no possibility of an eternal purpose for life. Life is valuable simply because it exists. Additionally, all life has naturally and purposelessly evolved from less complex forms. As such, human life is not innately more valuable than any other life form. All life is equally valuable. This leads to an understanding of the value of life which focuses on

the survival of the species rather than the fulfillment of a purpose for individuals.

As such, determining whether or not taking a life is acceptable is based on how it affects the survival of the society, not on any kind of objective morality. The result of this kind of thinking is that murder, abortion, and euthanasia may or may not be legitimate options depending on the particular situation. If society believes the taking of an individual life contributes to the survival of the species, it can be seen as good thing.

In general, the survival of an individual life is less important than the survival of society. When it comes to taking life, rightness or wrongness is determined by those in positions of power as they evaluate the benefit to the social order. This principle applies both in the private and the public arena.

It also extends beyond the life of human beings. Since no life form is more important than any other, some liberals also find it important to be advocates for other life forms. This becomes the basis for animal rights and environmental activism.

Chapter 14
Law

"Sally, come here and sit down. I have something I want to show you," Lance exclaimed as Sally walked toward the table. It was Thursday again and the two of them were meeting to have their regular weekly discussion.

Sally got to the table and scooted into her seat. She noticed that Lance had already ordered her drink. "Thanks for getting my drink for me," Sally offered. "And before we get into something else, I just want to thank you for the interesting discussion last week about evolution. Very provocative."

"Definitely my pleasure," Lance responded. "You know you are welcome anytime."

At that, Sally turned the conversation back to Lance's original topic and asked, "So, what are you reading?"

"I was doing a little research on the Supreme Court and came across this article about Stephen Breyer. You know who he is, don't you?" Lance asked.

"Of course I do." Sally answered back, "He is one of the most brilliant legal minds ever to serve on the high court."

"What? Brilliant mind?" Lance shot back. "He is the very definition of an activist judge. Look at this. It says, 'Breyer's pragmatic approach to the law attacks the very concept of originalism. Instead of using a more literal reading of the Constitution's text, history and tradition, he looks more closely to the purpose and consequences.' Do you see that? 'Pragmatic approach...' 'Attacks the very concept of originalism...' 'Looks more closely at purpose and consequences...' No, this is just not the American way."

"Whoa! Slow down, cowboy," Sally quipped back as she giggled under her breath. "This was going to be fun," she thought. "This really gets under his skin."

"What do you mean, 'slow down.' This is pure bunk," Lance shot back.

At that, Sally began to dig in. "Lance, the constitution is well over 200 years old. There is no way it can take into account all of the things that have to be dealt with in today's world. Judges have to have a little bit of leeway to address modern issues. That's just a fact."

"Fact, my eye," Lance shot back. "The constitution wasn't designed to be a document to give rights to the government. It is supposed to limit what the government can do. Besides, what it gives are principles for governing. Breyer and his cronies are interpreting based on their own beliefs and opinions. If judges operate that way, the meaning of the law will change every time there is a change in the judges. That's just not right."

"Just hang on a second." Sally cut into the argument. "You are simplifying things a bit too much. Judges who use a positive philosophy don't just use their opinion. They take into account the text, history, tradition, precedent, the purpose of a statute, and the consequences of competing interpretations. Don't you think that is a good, broad basis for making decisions?"

"No," replied Lance, "it is not. There is way too much room for personal opinion in your list."

"So," Sally retorted, "how in the world can you expect the law to keep up with the times? There are issues related to the internet and computer technology and modern transportation technology and medical technology and on and on that simply did not exist when the constitution was written."

"That doesn't matter," Lance replied. "The principles for making the decisions are all there. And besides, if the constitution needs to be changed, there is a legal way of doing it."

"Yeah, but that takes so long and is so complicated. In today's fast paced world, the legal system needs to be a lot more nimble," Sally countered.

"You're just wrong this time, Sally," Lance shot back.

But Sally wasn't going to let him get the best of her on this one. "No," she objected, "you are the one who is wrong here."

At that, Lance just shook his head in disbelief. "How in the world could anybody believe that," he thought.

From that starting point, Lance and Sally debated the rest of the mealtime about the pros and cons of the two very distinct approaches to understanding law. Finally, Lance looked at his watch. "Oh, I've got to get out of here. My conservative 'hayseed' leadership council is having a planning meeting I have to get to."

"Hey, get going. I'll pick this one up so I don't owe you anymore," Sally responded.

"Oh man," Lance retorted, "if I had realized that, I would have ordered the steak and lobster today."

They both laughed as Lance headed for the door. Sally thought, "Wow, that sure was intense."

****

Every society must have a set of rules which define acceptable and unacceptable conduct to maintain order in society. The topic of law relates to the particular rules society uses to promote order within the culture. The different worldview systems have different approaches for creating these rules. And as in all of the other areas, liberal and conservative approaches are based on entirely different ways of thinking.

Conservative Law

Conservative law begins with the assumption that God exists and has revealed his will about what is right and wrong. Therefore, conservatives believe that human law should reflect these instructions from God – at least in principle, if not in the specific laws themselves. Conservatives believe that God established the social order to operate in a particular way. He founded his system on an absolute standard which does not change. His system is, first of all, reflected in the laws of nature, and second is seen in the moral standards God has given to mankind through his revelation. This revealed law casts light on the true nature of humanity and on God's purpose for the advancement of society.

Conservatives believe that God's absolute standard exists not only in the natural order, but in the moral order, as well. This belief produces a legal system which does not fluctuate based on the whims of the day or the preferences of those in power. It is based on the belief that the unchanging God who created the natural universe also established a proper set of rules for society to follow which he revealed to mankind through the Bible. There is no human preference or whim associated with it. God has revealed the foundation of morality and it is up to human beings to take these moral principles and apply them in society by the creation of societal laws.

As a result, government's purpose is not to create laws. Rather, its job is to apply divine law to human society and properly enforce it. Government should encourage people to obey this law by punishing wrongdoers and protecting those who live rightly. A conservative understanding of law is founded on five basic precepts:

1. The source of all divine law is the character and nature of God.

2. The moral order proceeds from and reflects the character of God – his holiness.

3. Human beings are created in God's image and are, thus, significant.

4. When Jesus Christ took on human form, human life assumed even greater significance.

5. God, through Christ, will judge the whole human race according to his standard of good and evil.

Justice, Rights and Duties

Based on conservative ideals, one of the most significant implications of law in society relates to the concept of justice. The place where the emphasis of law is placed determines how justice is meted out.

God's revelation teaches that he created human beings in his image. This makes human life of highest value. Since conservative values put priority on the individual, the concept of human rights is of critical importance. Because of this priority, human beings have a right to expect true justice from their legal system.

Nevertheless, responsibilities come along with the rights and conservative values put limits on people's rights. Based on Christian Theism, conservatives expect human beings to act morally. This means that people have a duty to live their lives for God and to be obedient to the just laws of society.

Legislating Morality

While every law in existence is the legislation of some expression of morality, society cannot make every sin explicitly illegal. Morality and legality are not the same. A legal system based on conservative values attempts to legislate morality only to the extent that order is maintained in society and human rights are protected. The principle is to allow the expression of human freedom in every area of life to the extent that it does not threaten societal order. Additionally, the innocent should have no fear of the law while the guilty should have everything to fear.

Conservatives recognize that no legal system can make everyone act morally. Rather, law serves to create stability in society and promote justice as it sets boundaries within which society operates.

How Conservative Law is Expressed in the Culture
Impartial Judges

One of the key attributes of God, which is expressed in a conservative understanding of law, is fairness to everyone. One area where this must be expressed is in the judgment of the persons who are overseeing the legal process – judges. Conservatives expect judges to know the law and apply it impartially.

Fair Laws Which Apply Equally to Everyone

Another part of the fairness equation relates to the laws themselves. Just as the law of God is no respecter of persons, the laws of man should be the same. Conservatives believe no law should put any individual at an advantage or disadvantage related to others who live under the same legal system.

Due Process

Beyond the judges and laws, conservative law also insists that the legal process be fair. There should be a process which ensures fairness and consistency for every person dealing with the system. It should not favor one class of individual over another.

Beyond the individual, conservatives believe there should be consistency in the law itself. Once laws are created, judges and law enforcers should not interpret and carry out the laws in an arbitrary fashion. If changes need to be made to duly established laws, it should be done through a legal legislative process, not at the whim of judges and government executives.

Formal Accusations

Another part of the fairness equation relates to openness regarding the charges an accused person faces. Conservatives believe that if a person is charged with an infraction of the law, there should not be any uncertainty about what that entails. This helps ensure that the individual will be treated fairly.

Legal Trials

Another element of the legal process relates to how an actual trial is conducted. It is the governing authorities alone which have the power to enforce society's laws. Conservatives believe no trials should be conducted or punishments meted out which the government has not properly sanctioned.

Proof Beyond All Reasonable Doubt

Another element designed to ensure the fairness and integrity of the legal process is the necessity to demonstrate proof beyond all reasonable doubt when dealing with someone accused of a crime. Based on conservative values, true justice requires that the guilty be punished, but also that the innocent not be punished.

Restitution

Conservative law also promotes making amends when others are harmed. This is not only an element of fairness, but also of justice.

Liberal Law

Based on its naturalistic worldview foundation, liberal law is expressed in the principle of positive law. Law from a naturalistic worldview perspective has no objective or supernatural basis. Rather, it is established on the perceived needs of society and/or the personal inclinations of those in power. There is no other possibility. And, since there is no objective foundation for law, the laws themselves, and even the foundational principles for interpreting law, can be changed anytime based on contemporary circumstances.

Using this belief as a basis for understanding law, liberals do not recognize a constitutional document to be unchanging based on the intent of the writers. As such, it is subject to changing interpretations based on contemporary societal circumstances and the views of those responsible for doing the interpreting.

As liberals believe there is no God, no one is left but man to invent law and create order in society. This can only be done based on the beliefs of those who have the power to impose their will. The result is a system of laws which can be ever changing based on the whims of society and the personal preferences of those in power.

Liberal legal systems tend to put the highest value either on the desires of the ones wielding power or on the perceived needs of society in general. In either case, the rights of the individual fall below the needs of the collective.

Justice, Rights and Duties

One of the most significant implications of liberal law in society relates to how order is maintained within the collective. Keeping society orderly is of higher concern than the rights of individuals. Since liberal values put a priority on the collective, maintaining order is much more important than individual rights. It is the duty of citizens to recognize this fact and conform to the laws of society.

Legislating Morality

Based on liberal beliefs, morality is always relative to the situation. So, while every law is the legislation of some kind of morality, liberals judge the relative value of any particular act on how it affects society as a whole. A legal system based on liberal values is not as concerned with the notion of "morally proper legislation" as it is with "effective" legislation based on the current felt needs of the society.

How Liberal Law is Expressed in the Culture
Judges in Tune with Contemporary Societal Needs

For liberals, rather than fairness for the individual, order in society is the most fundamental value. As such, the key factor which judges must consider is how a particular case affects social order. Judges are the ones who must make these determinations. And since morality is situational, they can apply the law differently in different cases based on the situation.

Laws Which Promote Order in the Society

In liberal law, the most important concept for creating particular laws is not fairness, but order. As such, the laws themselves may be pliable to allow the most flexibility for the government to maintain order in society.

Due Process

Due process is not necessarily seen to be a bad thing, for liberals, in that it helps maintain order and consistency within the legal system. That being said, it is not absolute. If there is a need to cut certain corners to help maintain order in society, that can be done. Part of cutting corners can involve the approach judges use to interpret the law. Liberals don't see any reason why judges should have restrictions placed on their discretion as they interpret the law based on their understanding of contemporary needs.

Formal Accusations

Again, in the liberal conception of the law, formal accusations are not considered a bad thing, but are also not absolute. If the need arises for accusations to be hidden to promote societal order, there is no compelling reason that can't be done.

Legal Trials

Since moral relativism governs the liberal concept of law, there is no compelling reason why legal trials cannot be done away with in cases where there is a perceived threat to societal order.

Proof Beyond All Reasonable Doubt

Fairness is not the bottom line in liberal law. The most important principle is order. So if societal order is threatened, the principles related to proof and evidence may be altered to meet the current need.

Restitution

Liberal law sees no reason why restitution should be either necessary or unnecessary. This can be determined based on the circumstances of the case and how it affects societal order.

Chapter 15
Politics

As Sally was walking to the parking lot to leave campus, she heard what sounded like some kind of political rally. And sure enough, looking across the street at the city amphitheater, she saw a crowd of about 6,000 people at an anti-abortion rally. She had read that it was going to take place and that one of their state senators would be speaking, but was a bit surprised that it turned out to be this big a deal.

Then suddenly, over the loud speakers, she heard a voice that she recognized. It was Lance. "What was he doing being involved in that cause?" she thought to herself indignantly. "People who are against a woman's right to choose are just narrow-minded and mean spirited people." This really got her upset, so she decided to wait until he got through to give him a piece of her mind.

About twenty minutes later, the rally ended and she saw Lance finish greeting a few people and head over to his car in the parking lot. At that, she walked over there to confront him.

"Lance, what are you doing here?" she asked rather curtly. "Why would you participate in something like this?"

"Oh, hey Sally. Didn't expect to see you here. What's up?" Lance asked. He was genuinely surprised to see her and had no idea how upset she was.

"Don't 'what's up' me, Lance!" She exclaimed harshly. "I can't believe you would be involved in a hateful thing like this."

"Whoa! Hold on there," Lance shot back. "Why wouldn't I be involved in something like this? You can't mean to say that you are okay with the murder of innocent babies, are you? Don't you know that since the ruling in Roe vs. Wade, over 55 million innocent babies in America have been slaughtered? Of course I fight against that."

"Lance," Sally responded, "you conservatives have turned this into a political football when it should have nothing to do with politics. This is a health issue for women! It should be dealt with strictly between a woman and her doctor!"

"You are totally off the mark with this, Sally," Lance retorted. "This is not just about a woman and her rights. It is about innocent life being killed. And what do you mean it has nothing to do with politics? The initial ruling was purely the result of political maneuvering and the only way to correct this horrible wrong is through the political process. You do realize that we live in a democratic republic, don't you?"

"First of all, Lance, an unborn child is not yet a living person," Sally bristled back. "It is a potential person, sure, but has not yet achieved personhood. It is nothing more than living tissue at that point. It should have no rights, and what happens to it should be decided by the woman carrying it. It is her body that is being affected, after all. Still, I think you are turning a very personal and sensitive issue into a political one. That's just wrong!"

At that, Lance just shook his head and declared, "Sally, I don't mean to offend you here, but you are so emotionally jacked with this topic that you are not thinking clearly. How can you keep saying that this is not a political issue. It certainly is. In order to change things, we are required to act in the political arena. Those of us who believe abortion is immoral are having to support candidates who believe like we do. We are having to contact our representatives and tell them what we think. We are having to hold rallies like this one. But the truth is, people on your side are doing the very same thing. Are you saying that there is no politics going on with the pro-abortion side?"

"Well, there is," Sally hissed back, "but not because it is a political issue. It is because you conservatives are forcing us to do it. It is really a health issue."

"Well, in one sense that is true," Lance replied, "but it has to do with the health of an innocent baby, not the health of the pregnant woman."

This really was an emotional issue for Sally and finally she just turned around and walked off. She knew there was no reasoning with someone who held such irrational beliefs.

Lance hated to see her upset like this, but he knew that he could not back down from her. The lives of too many children were at stake.

****

Generally when people think of politics, the fighting between political parties and the posturing of politicians come to mind. But while there seems to always be an element of intrigue going on in the political arena, the actual work of politics is a bit more mundane. Politics involves the practice of administering states or other political units. It is the management of a governmental system. In the United States, the political system was set up as a democratic republic where the citizens elect government officials to carry out the will of the electorate.

Conservative Politics

The topic of politics is important for conservatives because they believe government is one of the institutions God established to help accomplish his purposes for mankind. Conservative politics is specifically based on Christian theistic concepts. This approach considers that God has revealed the moral principles which should govern society. Since conservatives believe God has ordained the work of government, citizens are charged with understanding his purpose and carrying out the work of government based on that purpose.

In the Bible, God has revealed two primary roles that a government should play. It is charged with protecting the innocent and punishing the guilty. In doing this it keeps order in society. It is the duty of politicians to manage government based on these principles.

In his revelation, God did not prescribe any particular form of government as the "right one." He did, however, give principals which point in a particular direction. America's founders recognized this and deliberately sought to figure out how best to create a governmental system which fit that mold.

The Need for Politics

Conservative political belief is based on the notion that the primary reason human government is necessary is because of sin. Human beings are inclined toward evil which, on a societal level, must be kept in check by laws and a government capable of enforcing them. So, in effect, an important purpose of government is to protect humans from their own sinful nature.

Along with that is the need to protect the citizenry from the sinful inclinations of those who hold governing power. The practice of dividing the government into three branches and imposing a system of checks and balances was specifically done to provide this safeguard. Making a distinction between the judicial, legislative and executive branches of government, as the American system does, promotes this principle.

The Source of Human Rights

Conservative politics is built upon the idea that the government is specifically ordained by God to protect the innocent and punish the guilty. This affirms the belief that humans are creatures created in the image of God. Based on this belief, conservatives affirm that the individual holds higher value than the collective.

This is partially expressed in the belief that God endowed man with certain basic rights. It is God himself who is the source and guarantor of these rights. Based on God's revelation concerning the value of human beings, conservatives believe government should be especially mindful of protecting and promoting human rights.

Ultimate Obedience

While God has commanded human beings to be obedient to the law so as to promote order in society, he does not consider humble submission to government to be unlimited. Conservatives recognize this and regard God's revelation to outrank human law. It is absolutely possible for the state to operate in ways which conflict with the commands of God. And when this happens, individuals are not duty bound to follow. Loyalty to God always supersedes loyalty to the government. If it comes to a choice of obeying God or the government, individuals are always to obey God, even if this means receiving adverse consequences imposed by the state.

How Conservative Politics is Expressed in the Culture
Relation of Government to the Individual

Conservative politics follows the biblical concept of the priority of the individual over the collective. As such, the government has a responsibility to operate in such a way as to guard life, promote individual freedom, and provide an environment where individuals can achieve their highest potential (life, liberty and the pursuit of happiness).

Human Rights

In conservative politics, the ultimate priority is the individual, not the collective. This is because God created man in his own image with a free will. When he created man, he did so with a specific purpose in mind which requires the exercise of free will. That purpose is for individuals to live in relationship with him. Conservatives believe the concepts of life, liberty and the pursuit of happiness express the sphere within which this becomes possible. As such, these become divine rights guaranteed by God himself. It is specifically the responsibility of government to make sure these rights are available to all citizens.

Civil Rights

Civil rights are those which belong to individuals simply because they are citizens. Based on a conservative approach to politics, this specifically includes such rights as due process, equal protection under the law and freedom from discrimination.

Civil Disobedience

Conservative politics firmly believes citizens should abide by the law of the land. If, however, laws are passed which violate an individual's conscience, conservatives believe that refusing to comply with the law as a peaceful form of political protest is permissible. This does not, however, relieve the individual from receiving the consequences of breaking the law.

Political Involvement

As the U.S. government was formed in a way which includes citizen involvement, conservatives consider it right for individuals to become involved in the political process. This rightness is based on the principle that oversight over the activities of government is part of a person's stewardship responsibilities under God.

In a democratic republic, there are many ways to do this. Involvement could include such things as running for office, helping people run for office, voting, expressing one's opinion to elected officials or in the press, advocating for laws and the like. Because of the particular structure of the American government, citizens themselves become responsible stewards of the political process. As such, conservatives believe that every citizen should be actively involved in politics at the appropriate level.

Liberal Politics

Liberal politics is based on the notion of a purely secular government. This concept rests upon a naturalistic worldview foundation which does not recognize the existence of a supernatural power or purpose. Because of this, politics is necessarily focused completely on an earthly outcome which promotes the ultimate goal of the natural order – the survival of the species.

The stress, then, is on the interests of the collective rather than on the individual. Since a communal mentality is the governing principle of society, politics is best expressed through some type of collectivist political form. The most popular collectivist approaches in our current time include, progressivism, socialism, and communism. Dictatorship is also a possible political expression of this naturalistic approach.

The Need for Politics

Since liberals do not believe there is any such thing as objective morality, the only restraints political leaders have on their power is that which is placed on them by the pressures of society or by their political competitors. They are, thus, free to exercise all of the political power they can manage to accumulate for themselves.

Those who agree with liberal political philosophy do not see this to be a problem as long as the politicians exercise their power in ways which promote the survival of the society. As liberals don't believe in the existence of any kind of objective morality, the means used to govern are not subject to an objective moral code. What is permissible is only constrained by what the population will allow.

Ultimate Obedience

Based on a liberal view of politics, submission to government oversight by the individual is of ultimate value. It is the governing authorities who ultimately determine the boundaries of what is morally acceptable. As such, it is the rigid duty of those within society to obey the government in order to promote the smooth operation and ultimate survival of society. Those who disobey rightly deserve to receive the full discipline of government power.

How Liberal Politics is Expressed in the Culture
Relation of Government to the Individual
Liberal politics is based on naturalistic beliefs which place the priority of the collective over the individual. As such, liberals believe the government's duty is to operate in a way which maintains order at all costs to ensure the survival of society. The rights of individuals are of secondary importance.

Human Rights
In liberal politics, the ultimate priority is the collective, not the individual. This is based on the belief that man is purely a physical animal whose highest value is survival. Based on this belief, the government's responsibility is specifically to promote that survival, even if it means trampling individual human rights in certain circumstances.

Civil Rights
The civil rights of individuals, in liberal politics, are not as important as the needs of the collective. Liberals believe, because of that, the civil rights of individuals may be set aside in particular instances if the situation justifies it.

Civil Disobedience
Liberal politics has no tolerance for civil disobedience. Since the collective holds priority over the individual, liberals see any actions which work against maintaining order in society as destructive and a threat to society's survival.

Political Involvement
Liberals generally see citizen participation in politics to be counterproductive to the smooth operation of governing. They believe that those in power are the ones best able to plan and carry out the actions which help ensure the survival of society. As such, politicians and government bureaucrats are granted the power and authority to manage the political process.

Chapter 16
Economics

The next Thursday, as per their usual arrangement, Lance and Sally met at the diner. Sally arrived first and went ahead and got their usual booth. Lance saw her when he walked in the door, headed straight for the booth and slid into the seat. "Hello, Sally," Lance offered as he tried to break the ice a bit. "I thought it might be a good idea if I wore some body armor today after our last encounter."

Sally laughed out loud. "Listen, I'm sorry I came across that way to you at the rally. I know you have different beliefs than I do about abortion and I really shouldn't have attacked you that way. I am just so passionate about that issue. Forgive me?"

Lance smiled back. "Yeah, no hard feelings. I'm pretty passionate about it myself."

"Hey," Lance continued, "did you see the economic numbers that came out today? Pretty devastating for your liberal president, don't you think? His socialist policies are taking us down a pretty bad path."

"Listen, I know that things are not looking so well economically right now," Sally answered back, "but you know full well that he inherited this mess. His policies are definitely going to turn things around if the stubborn conservatives would just get out of the way and let him implement them."

"Hey, if it weren't for those 'stubborn conservatives' you are talking about, we would already be in one of the worst recessions the world has ever seen. Even with the restraints being put on him, he is sucking the life out of the private sector faster than virtually any president in history. It is an unmitigated disaster. He needs to stop putting out all of those government regulations and free up the private sector to do its magic."

"What are you talking about?" Sally objected. "It is the greedy private corporations that got us into this mess in the first place. You have all of the rich fat cats preying off of the rest of society and just getting richer while the middle class is getting squeezed more and more."

"Sally, I know economics is not your area of expertise, but do you understand anything about it at all? Lance queried. "You simply can't keep running up debt and expect that it will not catch up with you at some point. You would never do that with your personal household budget and the very same principle holds true for the government. At some point a day of reckoning will arrive. You learn that in Econ 101."

"First of all, Lance, government finances are not like an individual's household budget. The whole system is different," Sally countered. "But beyond that, the government needs to regulate the economy. Since under capitalism the common man gets squeezed out, there needs to be a governmental system that can even things out. It's only fair. Why should rich people get all of the goodies?"

"Sally, do you even know what you are saying?" Lance responded back. It seemed, at that point, that the passion was beginning to build. "You are advocating a system where those who simply goof off in life basically live off the ones who work hard for a living. What's fair about that? A free market economy offers equality of opportunity. Everybody gets to go for the American dream if they want to. You are advocating for a system which promotes equality of outcome, no matter how much effort people put forth. I just don't see the fairness in that."

Sally could see that she really wasn't getting anywhere with Lance in this conversation and was getting a bit tired of his cheerleading for capitalism. "Listen Lance, your problem is that you just have a screwed up understanding of fairness. You need to spend a little time down at the homeless shelter or at the projects. When you see the difficulty those people face, it will change your attitude."

"Sally," Lance countered, "do you think I don't care about those folks? I contribute to our church's homeless ministry every month and even serve in it from time to time. I do care for those people. But you are never going to really help them if you make them dependent on the government for their existence. They need a hand-up, not a handout. They need an opportunity to get a job to provide for their families. That can't happen if you kill the private sector."

After another thirty minutes of back and forth, Sally decided she had heard enough. "Yeah, whatever!" she finally said. "Listen, I need to run. Let's pick things up again next week. I need a little space."

"That's cool," Lance responded. "I really do hope you have a great week. See you later."

With that, they both got up and walked to the front to pay their tabs. They were both thinking, "Sheesh, there is certainly no shortage of issues for us to talk about."

****

Economics is the study of the production, distribution, and consumption of goods and services within a society. It also deals with the attempt to understand economic systems and how to manage them effectively. The worldview platforms that conservatism and liberalism represent contain beliefs which affect how people conceive of economics – both in terms of value and methodology. The two systems have entirely different ways of dealing with this topic.

Conservative Economics

Conservative economics is based in the concept of the stewardship of property. It begins with the belief that God is the owner of his entire creation. Based on biblical teachings, the property individuals own is not really theirs. Rather, conservatives believe it is a sacred trust from God who is the ultimate owner. They believe individuals are responsible for managing the property in their care based on the desires and purposes of God.

In addition to physical property, conservatives also believe that God allocates gifts and talents to individuals. Using the same principle of stewardship, everyone is responsible to be productive with their own gifts and talents, as well as good stewards of the things they acquire which others produce. Conservatives measure the value of what is produced by how it is used to accomplish God's purpose in the world.

Economic Competition

Conservatives believe that the best use of gifts, talents and physical property is based on free market principles. Free market capitalism rests upon the notion that individuals should be allowed to freely exchange goods and services in a market where regulation is kept to a minimum. As a general principle, the Bible supports a system which respects private property. It also encourages individuals to act responsibly as God's steward with their property.

The Bible clearly teaches that workers deserve their pay and that those who work hard should be rewarded. By the same token, those who are lazy will remain poor.

Conservatives do not see capitalism, though, to be a means to promote unbridled greed. The biblical approach is to use capitalism in a way which encourages cooperation. As people produce specific goods and services of value to others, they benefit as they sell them. The benefit continues as they purchase goods and services produced by others. At the same time, society benefits as more resources are inserted into the market.

Economic Fairness

The conservative idea of justice is about equality of opportunity, not equality of outcome. Conservatives believe no one should ever be denied impartial justice under the law. By the same token, everyone should have the chance to succeed based on the stewardship of their gifts and talents, no matter their income or social status.

But this kind of equality does not guarantee equal results. Based on interests, gifts, life situation, effort, etc., some will achieve materially beyond others. This does not mean that the low achievers have been treated unfairly. In fact, many people purposefully choose professions which pay less because they value outcomes other than money. Fairness is not a matter of showing favoritism to the poor, but of providing equal opportunity for everyone to make their own way.

Conservatives believe that when capitalism is practiced in a way which is guided by Christian principles, the rich become the ones who aid the poor by helping to expand the pool of wealth. They do this by providing more jobs and a higher level of income for ever more people. It also provides a structure which allows those with more resources to help those in need.

A conservative approach to fairness considers that most, though not all, people who become and remain poor do so because of a wrong attitude about work, not because of a lack of opportunity to achieve. When injustice does exist which limits individual opportunity, the remedy is not to redistribute the wealth of those who have succeeded. It is to tear down the barriers to opportunity.

Freedom and Economics

Conservative economics promotes freedom. That is because a strong central government which controls the purse strings is not necessary. Citizens are free to produce and spend their own resources as they please. Using this model, the power lies more in the hands of the nation's citizens than in the government.

How Conservative Economics is Expressed in the Culture
Free Market

Conservative economics is founded upon the concept of a free market. It is based on the idea that God created human beings as purposeful, free-will individuals who are responsible for exercising their freedom in the world. A free market puts the responsibility for production and consumption squarely on the shoulders of the individual. God's purpose is that this production and consumption should be exercised by people who recognize themselves to be God's stewards. As such, conservatives live their lives in a way which leads them to use their resources to accomplish God's purpose in the world.

Equality of Opportunity

Since freedom is a key concept in conservative economics, no one expects that all people will end up with the same outcome. Individuals choose the direction of their lives, and these choices result in different outcomes. What is important for conservatives is not any particular outcome. Rather, it is the opportunity for people to go in whatever direction they wish based on God's guidance, and to produce to the best of their ability.

Personal Responsibility

Conservatives believe that true freedom requires an emphasis on personal responsibility. For that to happen, society must allow people to be fully responsible for the outcomes of their actions. This means allowing people to fail as well as to succeed in the various areas of their lives. When a person chooses to move in a particular direction in life, the result of that movement is not based on the merit or the fault of other people. It is strictly the result of the choices of the individual.

Charity

Conservative economics is based on biblical values. One of those values is to take care of our fellow man. Conservatives believe that individuals, rather than the government, should be responsible for meeting human need. As such, those with means should take it upon themselves to voluntarily help the needy.

Liberal Economics

Liberal economics is based in Naturalism and operates on the principle of interventionism. A naturalistic understanding of economics begins with the belief that there is no supernatural existence. As a result, liberals believe the only principles which exist to guide economics are those which society's leaders consider to be helpful in advancing the goals of human society. Again, the species (society) rather than the individual takes precedence. The tendency that emerges from that is an economic approach which promotes the welfare of society above that of the individual. This generally involves some kind of central guidance by those who control the purse strings of society.

Centralized economies are based on the concept that a group of central planners exercise control over the market and decide how to distribute goods and services. Liberals believe that having the economy centrally planned eliminates the problems of greed and envy, and avoids the messiness and disorder of any system based on the unrelated and unregulated actions of individuals.

Economic Cooperation

Cooperation, in liberal economic systems, comes in the form of collectivism. Liberals believe that all members of society should work in a way which promotes equal outcomes, no matter the particular work being done. They consider all work to be equally valuable to society, so all should receive the same benefits. In a liberal economic system, the government controls the means of production and distribution so, functionally, all workers are government employees. When people work, they turn a portion or all of the fruit of their labor over to the state to be distributed by the central authorities.

Social Justice

Liberal economics believes that social justice demands everyone share limited resources equally. That is, no matter how much or how little an individual produces, everyone should end up with the same amount. It is considered that "this is only fair." As such, there are no rich and poor. Everyone gets the same.

Based on the concept of social justice, wherever one finds a society with a poor lower class, liberals believe the poverty occurred because the rich have exploited the poor. As such, the poor don't have a chance because the rich keep them down. A redistributive model of economics overcomes this problem by taking the wealth of the better off and redistributing it to the less fortunate by manipulating tax rates or through tax breaks and government programs.

Freedom and Economics

Since liberal economics uses a small number of people to plan the economy and distribute the goods and services of society, a very strong central government is required. The people who run the government thus become all powerful and are assumed to be benevolent and to have a superior ability to make proper economic decisions. Individual freedom in this arena is unimportant and unnecessary.

How Liberal Economics is Expressed in the Culture
Collective Economic Model

Collectivism is the organizing principle of liberal economics. It is based on the idea that human beings are merely physical animals seeking to ensure their survival. A collectivist approach puts the responsibility for production and distribution of goods and services squarely on the leaders of society. Government officials have the responsibility of discerning society's needs and making sure they are met.

Equality of Outcome

Since community survival is the most important outcome, liberal economics operates in a way which attempts to insure that all people end up with the same result – despite position or effort. Liberals believe that as the government plans and implements actions which take care of everyone's needs, all problems related to inequality which could threaten the survival of society are eliminated.

Government Responsibility

Based on liberal thought, the best way to take care of the needs of society is through government control. This takes away the possibility that people will fail or that greed and envy will tear society apart.

Chapter 17
History

"Sally!" Lance blurted out as he approached the table. As was the usual case, Sally had arrived at the diner first and had already ordered their drinks. "I just read something that fits into your area of expertise and am interested in hearing your perspective on it."

"Oh yeah?" Sally replied. "What might that be?"

"Well, I was looking through one of my religion journals and it was dealing with the topic of history – more specifically, how God is working out his purpose in a historical setting," Lance began to explain. "Then I thought of you. You don't believe in God, so how exactly do you conceive of and teach about what goes on in history?"

"Well, of course you are right about my not believing in God," Sally responded. "And how I approach it is not really that complicated. History is nothing more than the non-repetitive sequence of events which happens in a linear fashion over time. In other words, as time moves from past to present to future, events happen. Human beings are able to notice and record these events, through various means, in order to pass that information down to future generations."

"I pretty much agree with your definition," Lance chuckled. "We need to mark this one down. We don't agree too many times."

Sally laughed out loud. "Yeah, I guess you are right on that one."

Then Lance continued, "But, of course, there is that one place where we diverge. I believe that the events which occur are expressions of a greater purpose – the purpose of God, himself."

At that, Sally smiled. Since this was her area of expertise, she felt like she had the upper hand in this conversation. "Lance, that just really doesn't make any sense. There are a couple of matters that even you must struggle with. First, in order for there to be a purpose, there must be someone present who can express purpose. I don't believe God even exists, so there is no one who is able to give a purpose to history in a macro sense. That being said, human beings can see some purpose on a personal level, and even a society can discern one. For instance, when someone gets their first job or gets married or something like that, those events have meaning for the individuals involved. People memorialize them by celebrating anniversaries. Societies do the same thing, like with the 4ᵗʰ of July or Christmas. Those events are meaningful for the society which celebrates them as meaningful, but there is nothing beyond that."

"You said there were a couple of matters involved. What is the other one?" Lance asked.

"The other issue related to purpose has to do with evil in the world. If God exists and history is purposeful as you insist, then God must be responsible for even the evil things which happen in the world. So, you have to consider that, for instance, God caused the destruction of the World Trade Center in order to accomplish his purpose."

"Not really," Lance replied back. "The fact that evil occurs in the world does not necessarily mean that God is the cause of it. In Christian belief, there is this thing called 'the Fall.' We believe that God created the world perfect but that based on a free-will decision, Adam and Eve disobeyed God in a way which allowed evil to enter the world. This created a situation where God's purpose was messed up. We believe that the rest of history has been the story of God working to redeem the fallen world to ultimately restore his perfect creation."

"Yeah, sounds like a fairy tale to me," Sally responded. "I just don't see it. Anyhow, I teach my students based on the assumption that God does not exist and that history has lessons for us, but the lessons relate at the personal and societal level – there is nothing else."

"You confirmed pretty much what I expected," Lance replied. "But thanks for your insight on the topic. You did a really good job of laying out your worldview belief on this."

"My pleasure," Sally replied back with a gleam in her eye. "I love talking about this topic. With my students, I pretty much only get to talk about the events in history. It is good to be able to get into the philosophical elements sometimes."

"Hey, don't mean to change the subject, but the administration is having that meeting next week to go over the changes they plan to make to the faculty handbook. Do you plan to go?" Lance asked.

"Oh yeah!" Sally answered, "I wouldn't miss it. Some of the proposed changes will be pretty important. They involve some significant alterations to the administrative philosophy of the school which will affect our teaching. You going?"

"Yeah, I'm going too. This one is too important to miss," Lance replied.

"Well good," Sally responded back, "I'll see you there and we can compare notes on how we see it."

At that, they both got up, paid their bills and headed out.

"See you next week, Lance."

"Great! You have a super week, Sally."

****

For some, it may seem that the concept of history would not be subject to different interpretations based on worldview. But, in fact, there are different ways to conceive of it. In fact, it is a critical element for understanding how human beings conceive of their place in the world. The particular way individuals understand history actually expresses the direction they choose for their lives.

Conservative History

The principle notion regarding the significance of history, in conservative thinking, is found in the word *purpose*. Specifically, conservatives believe that history is grounded in the purpose of God. They understand history as a purposeful, non-repetitive sequence of events which began in God's creative activity and is moving forward to accomplish his purpose for creating it.

Conservative beliefs do not see the work of God simply in spiritual terms. When God created the universe, he created an actual physical entity which moves through time to accomplish a purpose. Human beings live life in this physical world and their lives play out in a historical context.

Purpose in History

In the conservative view, history is not simply a meaningless linear sequence of events. An actual purpose is being carried out. This purpose began in the creation. God had a particular reason for creating the material universe, and that reason is connected to his personal interaction with human beings.

Conservatives believe God's purpose is exposed dramatically in man's Fall in the Garden of Eden. Before the Fall, God was fulfilling the purpose of his creative activity by actively interacting with man. But when the first humans sinned, that personal fellowship with God was broken and, in the process, God's purpose was spoiled. As the material universe had meaning and purpose to God, he began a redemptive process, which is being carried out in history, to reverse the effects of the Fall. This redemptive process was finalized in a historical event – the death and resurrection of Jesus Christ.

In order to understand the meaning associated with history, though, we must look beyond God's work in the past. There is also a future end that he plans to accomplish. His ultimate goal is to restore humanity to fellowship with himself. This fellowship not only makes history meaningful in a generic way, but to individual human beings on a personal level, as well.

Linear Conception of History

A conservative understanding of history is linear. Conservatives conceive of it as having begun in God's creation and moving forward through time toward a purposeful end. In the process of going from beginning to end, the events of history are following a non-repetitive course. This approach to history leaves us with a meaningful, goal-directed interpretation of history.

How Conservative History is Expressed in the Culture
Purpose in Human Life

Based on a conservative viewpoint, the purpose of God for humanity has a historical component. God especially created human life for his own purposes. As such, conservatives believe the lives of individuals are of ultimate value as they are lived out in time. They believe any action which degrades the value of human life is bad. This particularly includes such things as abortion, euthanasia (or assisted suicide) and murder.

Purpose in Historical Events

In conservative thinking, the living of life, itself, has meaning. There are two areas where this plays out. First, conservatives believe history is meaningful generically based on God's purpose for creating the material universe. Beyond that, they believe God has a purpose for each individual life. As people align their lives with God's purpose, they partner with him to accomplish his will in a historical context. This gives meaning to individual lives beyond what naturally happens within the flow of history.

Liberal History

Based on liberal beliefs, history has no meaning beyond that which human beings give it. That is because they do not believe there is any supernatural being above history who is able to assign a higher purpose. History becomes simply a record of the natural operation of the material universe. Liberals see mankind to be progressing to higher levels through history, but this is strictly the result of evolutionary progression as a natural animal.

Liberals also understand history to be linear in that it moves from past to present to future in a non-repetitive fashion. However, they see no overarching purpose associated with it since no-one exists to give it a purpose.

How Liberal History is Expressed in the Culture

No Purpose in Human Life

In liberal belief, there is nothing in existence to give an eternal purpose to human life. Any purpose that individuals experience must be personally created. As such, the primary focus of human interaction in history is to record events rather than understand purpose.

No Purpose in Historical Events

The movement of the universe through time occurs as a matter of physical reality without any purpose. The existence of purpose requires that there be a person to assign purpose. Since liberals do not believe in the existence of a supernatural God who is capable of overseeing history, there can be no overarching purpose in it. Thus, purpose in history only applies at a material level.

Chapter 18
Education

Lance knew the faculty meeting would be crowded today, so he decided to go a little early to get a good seat. But, lo and behold, when he arrived, he saw Sally already there. She was sitting by herself, seemingly absorbed in her own thoughts. Lance snuck up behind her and boomed in her ear, "Hey, anybody sitting here?"

At that Sally jumped straight up and whirled around. "You!! You scared me to death. What's the big idea?"

At that, Lance laughed so loudly that some of the others in the room looked over to see what was going on. "Get over here, sit down and shut up," Sally howled back with a stern look on her face. She then grabbed his arm and pulled him down into the seat next to her. Lance was still laughing, and when Sally looked in his face she couldn't help herself and started laughing, too.

"You're just mean," Sally snarled back at him with that embarrassed look on her face. "You know I will get you back."

"I know," Lance snickered, "but it will have been worth it."

Lance then pulled out the agenda and pointed at item number 4. "Have you had a chance to look at this yet?" he asked.

"Not yet, what is it?" Sally responded.

"You are probably aware of the new anti-discrimination policy the administration wants to implement," Lance continued. "Every club on campus would have to have its constitution approved by the school administration and they cannot discriminate regarding who rises into its leadership."

"So," Sally replied, rather surprised that Lance would have a problem with that, "what's the big deal?"

"What's the big deal? Think about it," Lance answered back. "Based on what has been happening on numerous other campuses around the country, this is specifically aimed at Christian clubs. They are going to insist that the leadership of even these clubs be open to anyone. How can you insist that people who are not Christians be allowed to lead a Christian club?"

"Well, I think it is only right for a campus club," Sally responded. "This is a secular university, after all, and we simply can't have any kind of discrimination going on here. In fact, that should be one of the cornerstones of our entire university environment – in the classroom as well as in university-sponsored clubs."

"Sally, do you have any idea what you are advocating?" Lance shot back. "You may not have much use for the Christian clubs yourself, but that also means you have to let Christians become leaders in your own precious Atheist club. What if a couple of dozen Christians decided to crash the party and basically take over the club? What would you think about that? And what about the other clubs? The Jewish club must allow non-Jewish leadership. The Islamic club must allow non-Muslim leadership. Sororities must allow in guys and the fraternities must allow girls. The Mensa club must allow those who don't now qualify. You get the idea. This could destroy every club on campus."

"Well, to make things fair, sometimes you just have to make those kinds of sacrifices," Sally responded.

"Fair! You call that fair?" Lance looked at her with an incredulous stare and shook his head.

Then it suddenly dawned on him and he slowly continued. "Ah, I am beginning to get it now. This fits so perfectly with your worldview perspective. You don't believe in God or any absolutes of any kind – even those associated with various kinds of groups. Even in the classroom your whole approach to teaching history is based on the premise that there is no such thing as purpose other than what human beings conceive. It follows, then, that no part of the education process teaches truth. Every expression of education, for you, is simply a means by which society 'socializes' the masses. Am I getting close here?"

Sally smiled and nodded her head in agreement. "You are, indeed, catching on, my friend."

Lance continued, "So, you see these 'exclusive' groups as being antisocial manifestations which need to be eliminated as a part of the educational process – especially at a secular university. Have I nailed it?"

"Lance," Sally replied, "you have such a refined way of explaining things. You have interpreted correctly. So, soon it will be time to vote to do away with all of the discrimination that exists in the various student organizations, just like we have been doing in the classroom."

At that, Lance truly got the picture and was crestfallen. Her very understanding of what is fair and right was so much different than his. "These worldview differences have much larger implications than I ever imagined," he thought.

Lance knew that the vote on agenda item 4 was coming up soon and that he would speak against it in as strong a terms as he possibly could. He also knew that he was very much in the minority and would probably not be able to stop it.

****

Education has two important components. First it is the process of conveying specific knowledge and skills to others. Secondly, it involves imparting good judgment and wisdom. The goal is to pass the important elements of culture from generation to generation.

Education is a lifelong process beginning at birth and continuing throughout life. It involves both formal and informal elements. Formal education is generally associated with participation in some kind of educational institution, while informal education is what people learn from other parts of life.

Conservative Education

Based on conservative thinking, the primary function of education is to pass on knowledge and wisdom from one generation to the next. The ultimate goal is for people to learn what is necessary to accomplish God's purpose in the world. Conservatives believe God created mankind for a purpose, and that he revealed that purpose in the Bible. His purpose involves a knowledge component and a personal component. As such, it is up to human beings to learn appropriate knowledge and pass it down to the next generation. On the other side of the equation, individuals must take that knowledge and apply it in life to accomplish God's purpose in the world.

Impartation of Knowledge and Skills

Based on conservative beliefs, the education process begins in the nuclear family as parents teach their children the right way to live. This part of the process is mostly informal as children observe how the world works from their platform within the family. There are also more direct educational efforts during this time as parents actively teach their children the things they need to learn as they grow.

For most people, education continues in a more formal learning environment as children enter their school age years. Beyond the basics of reading, writing, math, science and other foundational subjects, conservatives believe that a moral component should also be a part of the formal learning environment. The particular moral beliefs that children should learn are those expressed in the Bible.

Purpose in Education

For conservatives, education is not merely the acquisition of knowledge. It also involves the purposeful use of that knowledge. This purpose is based on the purpose of God as expressed in the Bible.

Since conservatives understand humans to be purposeful beings, they believe learning should not stop when formal education is completed. They believe that continuing to grow toward excellence throughout life is a biblical value and human beings ought to strive toward that end. As such, people should take the knowledge they learn and actually apply it in life. Simply having a body of knowledge stored in one's brain is essentially useless. The purposeful use of knowledge is critical to a faithful life and should be guided by the teachings found in the Bible.

How Conservative Education is Expressed in Culture
Individual Focus

As in all of the other arenas, conservatives believe the focus in education should be placed on the individual. It is individuals who are charged by God to achieve their highest potential. As such, the education process should be set up in a way which allows individuals to become the best they can be. This means that school curricula, as well as the actual structure for delivering education, should be set up in a way which promotes this end.

Human Development

Conservatives see the importance of education through the lens of God's purpose for humanity. Growth, as a person, is an important part of this purpose. The biblical revelation encourages individuals to strive for excellence in every part of life. Education, whether formal or informal, is an important means for accomplishing this purpose.

Conservatives view education as a lifelong process, not simply as the time a person spends in school. The foundation of that belief is that human beings are persons created in the image of God who are to grow in knowledge and wisdom throughout their entire lives.

Spiritual Development

Based on conservative beliefs, education is not confined strictly to intellectual knowledge. The proper application of that knowledge produces wisdom. Since conservative beliefs are based on a Christian theistic foundation, a proper application of knowledge is expressed in biblical morality. Conservatives characterize this process as growth in wisdom and also as spiritual growth. As was the case with intellectual development, conservatives understand spiritual development to be a lifelong process.

Liberal Education

Liberal education is based on the beliefs of Naturalism. As such, education's primary function is to promote the survival of the human race. Liberals believe that man is a chance accident of naturalistic evolution, so no objective purpose exists for any part of human existence, including education. As with the development of every other aspect of human culture, liberals hold that education is merely a useful tool for societal development and survival.

Impartation of Knowledge and Skills

As with conservatives, liberals recognize that the education process begins in the nuclear family as parents teach their children. In the case of liberal education, however, there is no recognition of any kind of "proper" morality children ought to be taught. Liberals do not acknowledge any kind of objective basis for morality, so the moral education they give to children is based on the social mores of the day.

The purpose of liberal education is to provide the collective with the skilled personnel it needs to promote survival. Based on liberal worldview beliefs, there is no compelling reason any particular person must advance in their level of education. The educational advancement of any specific individual is of little consequence.

Purpose in Education

For liberals, education is essentially the attainment of knowledge and skills. Its purpose is to promote the ability of society to survive and effectively advance into the future. There really is nothing specific beyond that.

How Liberal Education is Expressed in Culture
Collective Focus

The focus of liberal education is on the benefit it provides for the collective. It is the human race that holds the highest priority, not the development of the individual. As such, educational content and structure should be developed in a way which promotes the collective purpose. This will generally involve eliminating methodologies which do not promote collective ends, such as schools which encourage individual thought and homeschooling.

Human Development

Liberals see education as a tool for promoting the survival of the human race. As society needs people to work in order to take care of its needs, it becomes necessary for there to be a system of education to equip the workers. Satisfying the needs of individuals is not a major concern.

Socialization

A liberal approach to education is based on the priority of the collective over the individual. As such, individuals need to be socialized in ways which best prepare them to be good citizens based on the needs of society. The education system is an important part of this socialization process. As such, the governing authorities have a compelling interest in setting the educational requirements. They do this by establishing what curriculum will be used as well as the content of the curriculum.

Societal Control

As the collective is more important than the individual in liberal education, social control and conformity is the overarching purpose of education. As such, it is appropriate for the government to manipulate nontechnical knowledge in ways which encourage the people in society to be more compliant. What is important is not nearly so much the content of the curriculum as meeting society's needs based on the perception of the leaders. As such, teaching technical skills is most important so society will have the workers required to take care of its needs.

Part III
The Life of the Masses

Chapter 19
Where it All Leads

"So, Lance, what do you think," Sally asked as they sat eating their burgers at the diner. "After all of the things we have discussed, have I convinced you of anything?"

"Well, in fact you have convinced me of one thing," Lance responded. "I am more convinced than ever that your point of view has nothing to back it up. I don't see how you can possibly continue to hold a position with so little support. Don't you think it is about time for you to step away from the dark side?"

They both laughed out loud at Lance's comment. There was no question in either of their minds as to the strong-willed nature of the other.

Then Sally spoke up, "Lance, I respect the fact that you have strong convictions. In fact, that is one of the really attractive things about you. Not just that, but you are able to articulate your beliefs in a very winsome way. You don't disrespect the people you disagree with. But in spite of that, I just can't get past the fact that you actually believe God exists AND that he speaks in ways human beings can understand. There is simply no evidence to support that position. It just makes no sense at all."

"Sally," Lance responded, "you still don't get it, do you? Don't get me wrong, I have the same sentiment toward you. I appreciate your deep convictions and your advocacy for them. But if anyone's beliefs don't have evidence for support, it's yours. There actually is evidence to support my beliefs and I have spent the last several months explaining it to you. It is just that you are not willing to accept any kind of evidence that is not filtered through your naturalistic paradigm. Empirical evidence is not the only kind that exists, you know. And, in fact, your naturalistic beliefs are not supported by science either."

Sally was so frustrated by that last response. "Of course they are," she countered. "Since I don't believe in God, science is all I have to depend on."

"That is what is so insidious about what you believe," Lance answered back. "You think your beliefs are based on empiricism, but they are really not. There is no science to support your beliefs about the origin of the materials that make up the natural universe. There is no science to back up your beliefs about the origin of life or the origin of human self-awareness. Your whole worldview is based on faith."

"You still don't get it do you, Lance?" Sally countered. "Just because we don't yet know the science behind those things does not mean we will not figure it out."

"That is my point," Lance replied. "You have faith that you can ultimately figure it out by science, but you hold that belief as a religious doctrine, not as a scientific one."

"You really are hopeless, Lance," Sally responded. "You realize that don't you?"

He answered back, "Yeah, to you I guess I am hopeless. I just thought that by now you would have seen the light."

"Listen, Lance, I have really enjoyed our conversations but I think that we have taken this about as far as we can," Sally replied. "I think I need a little break. I'm sure we will see each other a good bit around campus, but let's take a break from these weekly get-togethers, okay?"

At that point, Lance was pretty much feeling the same way. "Yeah, I think you are right," he responded. "This has been very productive in a lot of ways, but it probably does need a break. Maybe in the future, if some particular issue comes along, we can have a special pow-wow."

As they parted company, they were both experiencing a little sadness to see it end, while at the same time feeling a bit relieved to get a break. It had been a fascinating exchange.

****

Where Are the Lines?

The most difficult part about understanding the distinctions between liberal and conservative ideas is not the surface expressions.

This element is fairly clear. Rather, the difficulty lies in identifying the underlying sources which give the beliefs meaning. Many people who consider themselves conservative hold liberal positions on some issues. In the same way, many who consider themselves liberal hold certain conservative positions. This creates a situation where people who self-identify as either conservative or liberal disagree with others who self-identify the same way. Hopefully, getting at the sources of conservative and liberal beliefs has helped sort much of this out.

But because there is so much hybridization, the lines between conservative and liberal, on the surface at least, become blurred in many cases. That is why it is so important to get down to the level of worldview foundations in order to understand where the different beliefs come from. Liberal expressions in America come from Naturalistic worldview presuppositions, despite how any particular individual may label him or herself. By the same token, conservative expressions come from Christian Theism, no matter how a person self-labels.

Pop Culture Tends Toward Liberal Beliefs but Depends on Conservative Ones

In American society, the popular culture operates primarily from liberal worldview beliefs. This does not mean that all of the people who participate in the pop-culture lifestyle and enjoy the tastes of the majority self-identify as liberals. There are plenty of people in that category who consider themselves conservative. That being said, for the most part, the music, art, TV shows, movies, advertising, and the like, in popular culture, reflect values which come out of Naturalism, not out of Christian Theism.

At the same time, pop-culture depends on the existence of values from the conservative side. There needs to be disposable income and hard-working individuals who take personal responsibility seriously in order to create the products which become the consumables of those who participate in the pop culture. The two sets of values have become so intertwined that it is almost impossible to pull them apart.

We Want Our Cake and Eat it Too

Many consider the ultimate outcome of pure conservatism to be too straight laced. Conservative values promote hard work, personal responsibility, independence, responsible handling of money, good stewardship of resources, biblical sexual morality and other values that require people to voluntarily place restrictions of thought and action on their lives. At the same time, it holds a negative view of many activities which society embraces, and purposefully avoids them as they are considered "sins."

Pure liberalism, on the other hand, promotes an entirely different set of values. It often validates laziness, shifting of responsibility to others, dependence, selfishness, pride, and a lack of financial responsibility. This happens because there is no overarching purpose for life, no such thing as objective morality, and personal fulfillment is the highest purpose individuals can aspire to.

It is not that conservatism requires a "straight laced" life, but many who desire to participate in certain lifestyle activities which go against core conservative values perceive it that way. By the same token, it is not that liberalism requires a hedonistic lifestyle. It is just that liberalism provides the opportunity for it more readily. As such, many people select their core values based on personal desires, then mix and match to suit their lifestyle preferences. When that happens, the lines between liberal and conservative become blurred.

Another important point to remember is that a person's worldview, which is the ultimate source for values and lifestyle, is generally unconscious. Individuals don't usually recognize, at a conscious level, what particular actions emerge out of what worldview beliefs. As such, this mixing and matching is very easy to do. There will, occasionally, be times when people feel, at an intuitive level, the inconsistencies of mixing and matching. That being said, human beings are perfectly capable of living with those kinds of inconsistencies. Unless a person takes a conscious, principled stand, he or she will simply do what feels good at the moment.

Possible Hybrids

The hybridization of people's beliefs can take many different forms. Most of the time these forms end up with less than desirable results.

For example, a consistent conservatism, based on its theistic roots, will promote fiscal conservatism and biblical social values. Hybridize that, though, and you can end up with a type of fiscal policy which has a conservative veneer but promotes greed and selfishness to an extreme. We sometimes see this with certain businesses which are willing to act unethically in order to make larger profits. Another hybrid possibility would be to advance conservative fiscal policies but personal moral values which promote hedonism. Examples of this lifestyle are constantly in the news as many in the entertainment industry do all they can to maximize their income but are also known for their partying.

On the other side of the ledger, consistent liberalism would be a truly communistic society in which there are no class distinctions of any kind. Everyone would work as hard as they could and all receive equal outcomes. This kind of utopian desire, though, has never worked in real life.

There are several possible hybrids that may occur with a liberal slant. One might be where the political leaders become a privileged class above the workers. This is the situation which existed in the former Soviet Union and what we see even now in Communist China. Another hybrid would be a soft socialism where private enterprise still exists, but taxes are very high on the productive members of society and the wealth is redistributed to the less productive members through tax policy. Most of Western Europe is in this situation today.

American Reality

The current expression of conflict between conservatives and liberals in America has put us in a place of very sharp division. This can hardly be avoided in the end. After all, the core values of the worldviews these viewpoints are founded upon plainly contradict one another. In order for compromise to occur, individuals literally have to compromise their most deeply held worldview convictions.

This is not to say that compromise is impossible. But, at the level of worldview beliefs, compromise is not simply a matter of normal give and take. The only way to compromise worldview beliefs is to hybridize. Over time, this is exactly what has happened in American culture. So, what we have ended up with is a system which contains many internal contradictions. Along with that, any attempt to clear up the contradictions (which means promoting more purely conservative or liberal beliefs) will entail pushing against opposing beliefs at a worldview level.

The current situation in American society has the adherents of both sides in fairly even power situations. As time goes on, one side or the other will get the upper hand and press for policies which are more consistent with their beliefs. In recent generations we have seen this go back and forth many times. The only way to truly clear it up is for one side to totally convince the other to convert to different worldview beliefs. Until that happens, America's 21st Century Civil War will continue to be fought in every part of society.

Appendix

Overview of the Basic Worldviews

Naturalism
Basic Assumption: There is no supernatural existence. The only thing that exists is matter which is eternal and evolving.

Theism
Basic Assumption: There is an infinite and transcendent (supernatural) God who is the Creator and Sustainer of the material universe.

Animism
Basic Assumption: The universe contains both material and immaterial parts. Spirits exist in a separate place from physical beings, but they interact with each other in a symbiotic relationship. Humans on earth offer sacrifices and perform ceremonies which benefit the spirits, and they, in turn, take care of the needs of humans on earth.

Far Eastern Thought
Basic Assumption: The essence of all existence is the impersonal life force. There are pieces of that life force which are not merged with the central core, but which are constantly working their way toward it with the ultimate goal being to merge with it. All of life in the physical universe is nothing more than pieces of that life force which are working their way, through successive material incarnations, toward unity with the main body. The process is for the life form, at whatever stage, to live its life the best is can. If it does well, it will move up to a higher form in its next incarnation. When it makes it to the highest level and does well, the material reincarnations will cease and the life force merges with the impersonal main body. The essence of this worldview is pantheistic and monistic.

Hybrids
Hybrid is not, strictly speaking, a worldview category. It is the attempt to take elements from two or more worldviews and combine them. But since every worldview literally contradicts every other worldview, every hybrid belief system contains irreconcilable contradictions.

Topical Overview

Theology
The study of God.

Philosophy
The study of reality, knowledge and values.

Anthropology
The study of man.

Sociology
The study of human social behavior.

Psychology
The study of the soul.

Communication
The study of the way human beings convey meaning to one another.

Ethics and Morality
The study of moral principles and rules of conduct.

Biology
The study of life or living matter.

Law
The study of the particular rules society uses to promote order within the culture.

Politics
The practice of administrating states or other political units.

Economics
The study of the production, distribution, and consumption of goods and services within a society.

History
The study of past events.

Education
The process of conveying specific knowledge and skills to others. The impartation of good judgment and wisdom.

About the Author

Freddy Davis is the president of TSM Enterprises. He is the author of numerous books and has a background as an intercultural consultant, entrepreneur, radio host and religious worker. Freddy is a popular speaker, particularly on the topic of worldview and its practical implications. He lives in Tallahassee, FL with his wife Deborah.